A MEMOIR

MY LOVE AFFAIR WITH HARLEM STREET LIFE
AND THE MEN WHO RULED IT

MS. TEE

ROYAL-T
PUBLISHING

Copyright © 2015 Ms. Tee

All rights reserved, including the right to reproduce this book or portions hereof in any form whatsoever without written permission.

Note: Sale of this book without a front cover may be unauthorized. If this book was purchased without a cover, it may have been reported to the publisher as "unsold" or "destroyed," neither the author nor the publisher may have received payment for the sale of this book.

The events are portrayed to the best of Tonia Taylor-Bragg's memory. While the stories in this book are true, some names, and identifying details have been changed to protect the privacy of the people involved.

Published by

Royal-T Publishing, LLC
PO Box 600
New York, NY 10030
Email: **Royaltypub@gmail.com**

ISBN 10: 0692396888
ISBN-13: 978-0-692-39688-9

Harlem Heroin(e) Credits:
Written by: Ms. Tee
Edited by: Salih Israil and Ms. Tee
Cover Concept: Tonia Taylor-Bragg

Thank You

I want to thank everyone who stood by and supported me while writing this book. I want to thank them for their blessings. To my sister Shanda, aka Boop, you are my baby girl. You have been through everything with me. Mommy only gave birth to you. You were and still are my baby. You have seen it all. You were always there when I needed you. Even though we're six years apart, since you were a child we've been inseparable. You are my best friend. I love you.

To my big sister Janine, Thank you. To my mother, my world who worried many nights, but knew the power of prayer, I LOVE YOU LADY.

To my daddy, Jamaica's finest. R.I.P. You always taught us to be leaders.

To Tiana, mommy's angle. You are my world, the air in my lungs and the reason I do what I do. I love you and will always be proud of anything you do.

To my nephews Chris, Terry Jr., I love you.

To my niece princess Rhyan, I love you.

To my other brothers, sisters, nieces and nephews, I love you guys.

To my brother-in-law Mel, I love ya. You are a good dude.

To Lou, thank you for your love, support and helping me with this. You have been awesome.

To my uncle Stan, with ya big head, thank you. You never told me no and maybe that was the Goddamn problem. LOL

To Unique, thank you for your blessings. You have always made us smile. Thank you for a Good MF time.

Maine I love you man. You were my motivation 10 years ago. Thank you "Baby Jay." R.I.P

To Shelli, my partner in crime, we have done some thangs. Love you to pieces.

To my GG's, Love ya'll.

To my friend/sister/twin April Pringle. R.I.P. You'll live in me forever. GG for Life!

To my baby daddy, the one and only Ace, thank you so much for your support and the info. I know you got ya feet kicked up lying in the sun kid.

To Demetrius, thank you.

To Marquette and Salih, thank you for everything. You guys were the wheels that kept this machine going. I appreciate you guys so much. Thank you again. My feelings really can't be put into words.

To the Almighty, my Lord and Savior Jesus Christ, who has spared my life of many occasions, thanks for your Grace and Mercy.

Last, but not least thank you to the *Hood*. Not so much the people, but the experience. You have made me the strong woman I am today. If it weren't for you this book would not exist. You have introduced me to some wonderful people and some crazy ones too. SMH. We've been through a lot together. We have had good times and bad times. You stuck with me through thick and thin. I love you for the experiences. They will be long remembered. There is no college degree in the world that could have given me what you have given me.

TO THE FALLEN: Unfortunately there are so many to name. Rest In Peace, Some of you left us far too early. GOD Bless.

Harlem Heroin(e)

PROLOGUE

It's not my intentions to glorify the street life in no way shape or form. It was just my reality at a time in my life. This isn't just another one of those made up hood stories. The fact is that for most of my young life I was surrounded by and/or involved with people who were involved with the "street life" on some level.

Most of my relationships were with alleged killers and hustlers. Did I plan it that way? **No**. Do I wish things could have been different? **Maybe**. Do I have any regrets? **No!!** Let's just say that I'm disappointed about a few things, but I have no regrets. My environment made me the strong woman I am today.

Ten years ago I began putting the events of my life on paper. Yes 10 long years. This story is about what Harlem was to me and my experiences. It's my truth. There may be someone that has their own version of how things were to them. I'm not the only one with a story. There are hundreds of "Real" hood stories out there and some quite interesting too.

This is a true story about my life in Harlem and the life of a lot of girls from the hood that desired to be with men that led a not so desirable lifestyle. Well to some people (police, church folk, the government, etc.) it would be considered undesirable. To us it was **"THE LIFE"**. My environment was filled with sex, drugs, money and murder. That was Harlem.

For those of us who wanted the life, we probably got more than we bargained for. But we lived through it. Some of us survived it and some weren't so lucky. Although I've been shot inches away from my spine, tied up and robbed at gunpoint another time, and under investigation, I happen to be one of the lucky ones. I know you're wondering what was lucky about all that... **I'M ALIVE and FREE**.

For those females who think or thought they wanted to be a hustler's wife or be affiliated with "the life", it wasn't always what it seemed. For those dudes that are still trying to hang on to what use to be, it's **OVER**. For those who never got that chance to experience that life, consider yourselves lucky.

Many street legends have preceded us in death. A lot of my people didn't make it. Many of those deaths were senseless. But that's what "the life" was all about.

Some names have been changed, but the stories are real. The words **alleged** and **allegedly** will occur often in this book for obvious reasons. Besides the fun I had growing up in Harlem, my reason for writing my story is to **Inform, Enlighten, Enrich, Empower** and at the same time **Discourage** young men and women who may be thinking about adapting to the lifestyle of being a hustler or hustler's wife. It's also for those who wonder what it was really like. One thing I can say for sure is that- **IT'S OVER**... "THE GAME", "THE LIFE" is over. **Let it go. Times have changed and things are much different.**

It's time to be legit….. Go hard or Go home…... It's time to preserve the Black family.

Let's Talk.

JUNE 2000
PRINCE OF HARLEM
aka Baby Jay

Although a lot of my story starts way back in the 80's, I have to start with the year 2000. I mean, I had seen and been through a lot of stuff in the streets before then, but on the night of June 23, 2000; my life changed forever. It was a clear and beautiful Friday night, a couple of days into summer. I was home looking for something to wear to the club. I picked out a linen dress and some black sandals. Me, my sister and my brother Maine and his people were hitting this club downtown called Blue Angel, I think. We'd been hitting that spot for the last few weeks. That's how it was in Harlem back then. A spot started poppin' and that's where everybody went until dudes got stupid and forced the owner or the police to shut it down. It didn't matter though, because Harlem always found another spot. We'd make it hot and then some asshole would spoil it for everybody once again. But hey, that's the way it was.

Anyway, I called Maine up that night before I left the house. "What's up for tonight? What time ya'll gettin' to the club?"

"Sis, we chillin' tonight," he answered. "I think that kid Memphis Bleek is having a party there."

"Alright then, me and Tee Tee are going to get something to eat," I told him, referring to my daughter. She was eight at the time and since I wasn't going to the club, I decided to take her out to dinner. We went to Amy Ruths Soul Food on 116th Street. The food there was slammin'.

You know how people say they get bad vibes when something just doesn't feel right? Well, I didn't get that, but the next phone call I got caused excitement, fear and brought so much pain to my heart that I couldn't think straight. I hopped in my car and raced uptown to 5th Avenue and 133rd Street and found everybody standing around with looks of fear and pain on their faces. I also saw looks of shock

3

and surprise. It had happened so fast, Maine never knew what was waiting for him in the darkness. The boogieman was waiting and Maine never even had a clue.

It's crazy how someone can have control over your destiny and you don't even know it. It might as well have been a ghost that got Maine. It appeared in the night and disappeared just as quickly. Its intentions were to kill and destroy and that's exactly what happened. It killed Maine and destroyed the rest of us.

Someone out there told me that Ken threw Maine in the Escalade and took him to Harlem Hospital. I raced over there and stood in the lobby thinking about the first time I saw Maine's handsome little face as a young kid. I wanted to go back to those days, the days when he was happy and having fun. That's the only thing I wanted to think about. I didn't want to think of anything else. I didn't want to hear anything but his laughter in my mind. I didn't want to see anything except the images of his smiling face in my mind. I just wanted to hear him say "Tee" or "Sis" again. I wanted to see him walking out of that hospital. That's all. That's all I wanted. I just wanted Maine back.

****

Whenever I think about what happened to Maine, whenever I think about losing him, I can't help but to think about this one dude. I knew this dude and his family since he was young. HE was always a cool kid. HE went to school with my little sister. I went to school with one of his older sisters. HE did pretty well at school too. HE loved basketball and got along with everybody. HE was a lovable little guy with the cutest dimples.

HE and I remained cool over the years. HE eventually became a rapper, got down with a major record company and infamously became known for wearing shiny suits. LOL. HE also started a record label of his own and was successful with it. We saw each other from time to time. HE tried to holla once, but HE was still like a little cousin to me. HE cracked me up. We both got a kick out of it. You know how it is when dudes start getting money. They start thinking they can get anybody. It was cute though.

I think the last time I spoke to him was in 1997 after Biggie got killed. HE called me and we talked for a long time. That experience scared the shit out of him.

"I'm never going back to L.A.," I remember HE kept repeating.

I know he's been back since then, but at the time I understood why he felt that way. I would've felt the same way.

HE and Maine knew each other, but I really don't know how well. One thing's for sure, as kids growing up in Harlem, neither of them knew their lives would eventually cross in an unimaginable way. Neither of them could've known that so much tragedy, death and destruction would consume their lives; making one of them seek GOD and the other actually see GOD.

Theirs was a feud I will never ever forget. It's going on fifteen years since Maine's death and I wish that whole beef never happened. My heart ached for years. It still aches, but it doesn't ache as bad as it did back then. It aches to know that Maine's daughter will never really know how funny and how sweet he was. She's older now so I'm sure she hears the stories, but it's not the same as her being able to witness her wonderful father firsthand. I guess it's good that she can at least look at photos and see how handsome he was. I mean, my heart doesn't just ache for Maine. My heart also aches because two of the other victims of this feud were friends of mine too, even though the beef kinda' divided us.

This started with Maine and HIM, and it could've ended there. But when you're not strong enough to stand on your own and you enlist others to hold you down, this was the result. SIX DEAD!!!!! Some people wanted to blame Maine for this. NAH!!! He just chose to take on whatever came his way. HE should have done the same thing. The result could've been two men standing with their issues resolved or one man left standing. Those of you who know, probably know who would've been the one left standing. I'm just saying. That being said, I would've definitely stepped in and hopefully both would've been able to step off with their issues resolved. I loved Maine, and HE and I were cool enough for that to have been done. He could've contacted me, but I truly believe HE allowed others to influence his actions and decisions. Maine was no saint by any means, but he would've listened to reason.

I wish we could go back to the old days when men fought, got up and went home. Someone had to win and someone had to lose. Sometimes it was a real good fight and we called it a tie. Black men have to learn how to let things go. They must realize what's more important. They care too much about what the next person thinks. They're scared to lose a fight. More importantly Black men need to learn how to talk and resolve their differences like MEN. They care more about egos and impressing others than preserving life.

No one won this fight. Everyone lost in this feud. When it was all said and done I asked the question, "Why?" Why did six people have to lose their lives? What was it really over? Jermaine's death has been the discussion in magazine articles, among rap industry insiders, and on Hip Hop related radio and internet programs. All these people speculate about what happened. But do they really know? Do they know how many people were killed because of this beef?

What was the beef really over? Could it have been prevented? MAYBE. Why did HE really leave New York? Was HE involved in Maine's death? Why did HE really seek out GOD? Was it because HE felt guilty about something?

Maine's departure from this earth is what turned my life around. He's the reason why I put pen to paper. It's what made me realize that I had some unfinished business in my life and that I needed to get right with GOD. Without him, the "Street Life" wasn't fun anymore. Death caused too much pain. After a few years of dealing with the pain of his loss, I felt like I was losing control. I was stressed over the fact that there was nothing I could do to bring him back.

I ended up leaving New York in 2006. The years had taken a toll on me. I felt like the walls were closing in on me. It had been five years since Maine died, and I still had no control over how I felt. I needed to get myself together and I realized there was something that I did have control over, **MY LIFE.**

Again, the night of Maine's death changed my life forever, but the truth is that Maine was actually the last of a long line of real, smart and handsome street dudes I encountered along the way. Now I'm going to take you on a journey back to my life on the Streets of Harlem, a journey that intertwines the stories of many Street Legends. You may have heard about many of the street beefs in Harlem in the 80's and 90's, but I was there for some of them. I had a firsthand look at who was who and what was what, and this is my story. From the big-time hustlers and gangsters from back in the day, all the way to Maine and his crew, get ready for an inside look into what Street Life was really like in Harlem.

And by the way, I'll get back to Maine's story later, but first we have to take it back. Way back.

1985-1986
My Infatuation
with the Fast Life

Harlem was poppin' in the mid-eighties. Everybody from the Bronx, Brooklyn, Queens and from out of town wanted to be a part of Harlem. If it was a popular restaurant, they wanted to eat there. If it was a party, they needed to be there. Dudes from other boroughs envied dudes from Harlem. Yes, ya'll know ya'll did. Don't front. But let's be clear, there were definitely other reasons why Brooklyn showed up. Yeah, they were trying to take something back to Brooklyn with them, but it wasn't just girls or party memories. When those Brooklyn dudes came to Harlem, some Harlem dude was going home that night without his chain, Rolex watch or wad of cash. Ya'll know how BK was back then. They almost got me once. I had on a $150k cross and chain flooded with diamonds and my friend Arty peeped them scheming on me and made sure I got out of the spot untouched. Those MF's came just to see who looked like money. SMH!!

Harlem dudes had a certain type of swagger. We didn't use the word swag back then, but it was in full effect. Their hustle game was tight. It was all about looking fly, gettin' bitches, flashing the flyest jewels and non-stop flossing. They kept the latest cars, their gear was tight and the chicks loved it. Every crew was game tight, even the Jamaicans on Edgecombe Avenue. My girls and I couldn't get enough of being spoiled by them. Mmmmm Hmmmm. Harlem was about getting money. Who wouldn't have wanted a piece of that action?

As much as Harlem was about gettin' money, it also had the spots where you could show off the money you were getting. Rooftop skating rink was one of those spots. It was the size of somebody's living room, maybe a little bigger, but it stayed packed.

Rooftop was definitely a place to see who was who. And the music was off the hook. Shout out to Brucie B.

Amateur night at The Apollo Theatre was another place to show up dressed to impress. Everybody stood under the marquee's bright lights, breaking their necks to be seen. Wednesday nights were poppin' at the Apollo. In the summer the guys came through with their linen suits and gators on their feet and the girls came through in expensive designer wear with all the accessories. And when the winter cold came, the furs came out. You really had to be there to understand what I'm talking about. It's different now. Words can't really describe the atmosphere of the Rooftop, the Apollo, the Rucker, and of course Willie Burgers, which was open all night. Even though Willies gave me food poisoning one time, it was still good. If you didn't go there to eat, you definitely went there to post up under those bright lights to see who was out there, or to be seen. I must say we were some frontin' ass MF's in Harlem. Just thinking about it cracks me the fuck up. Ya'll saw the movie Paid in Full, right? Yep, that's just how it was.

There was also the S&S club and the Zodiac. Those were after hour spots. A lot of coke sniffing went on up in those spots, allegedly. I never went in those spots. I heard they use to be poppin' though. I use to be in this bar up on Broadway called Oasis with "Zip". Eric Von Zip that is. He was like Harlem royalty. One of my girlfriends and I hung out with him a lot. She was messing with him. I was there for the drinks. Zip had a friend who liked me, but he was too old and I wasn't about to mess with his old ass. He claimed one of the rappers from "Whodini" was his son. Til this day I'm not sure if he was telling the truth.

Zip use to take me and my girl to another bar down on 115th Street and 7th Avenue called the Blue something, or maybe the outside was blue. I can't remember. Either way, we had a good time with him. He just liked to have fun, talk shit with his people, and laugh. But let me get back to that Harlem street life.

Harlem guys always drove something fly. Back then there were the Saabs, the Alfa Romeos and of course the Benz' and the BMW's. My favorite car was the 740i BMW. I liked it so much I had my friend Troy Ryan from Drew Hamilton spray paint one on a white sweatshirt for me. Now I have to say as much as I loved

9

Harlem, once in a while, but not often at all, my girls and I ventured out to other boroughs to see what was going on. I remember this hot club opened out in Queens. I think it was the early nineties, I'm not sure. It was called Metropolis I believe. It was huge, but I don't think it stayed open long. I remember walking through the crowd with my girls and feeling someone grab my jacket. I turned around, and who did I see? Jigga, yeah Jay-Z. I just looked at him, nodded, and kept walking. My friends thought I lost my mind for not talking to him. He was Jay-Z, but of course he wasn't the Jay of today. At that time I'm sure I probably had a man that had just as much money and status as he did, if not more. But damn I do reminisce about what could have been. LOL. My point was that people didn't just come to Harlem, we took Harlem other places too.

Those were days we'll never get back, but we had fun though. We had a ball. Those were the days of the name belts, big ass rope chains and the four finger name rings. Todays' generation can't understand what it was like. It's too much recklessness with these young kids today. A lot of them feel like they've got nothing to live for. They think they know what hustling is, but they don't. It wasn't all fun and games back then, but it was better.

Back then it was love in the streets everywhere. Every avenue had a clique that was getting money. Blocks like 112th & St. Nick (Fritz block), 132nd & 8th (Big Stan, The Twins), 132nd & 7th (AZ, Rich Porter), 127th and 8th (Tee Money), 129th Madison (Ace), 129th Lenox, 116th Street, Manhattan Avenue, 132nd & Madison Ave, 159th & Amsterdam, 145th & Edgecombe, 144th & 7th Avenue, 143rd Hamilton Place, 145th & St. Nick. You get the picture. Harlem was hot. I'm sure all of us ladies that were out back then made sure we passed a few of those blocks trying to get somebody's attention.

Let me take it back. Do ya'll remember the jams in the parks and on certain blocks? That's when Harlem was fun. The DJ's would bring their equipment out and set up, and the dancers would set it off. My friends and I use to walk around to all the blocks that were jamming to see who was dancing and who was out. I remember when Tina Marie's song Square Biz came out. I was around 12 back then. I remember my boyfriend Eddie Allen had to be in the house when it got dark and I would sit upstairs with him listening to the music coming from St. Nicholas Park. Those were the days. Shout out to Disco Pam who was at every block jam gettin' it in.

That's when times were fun. The youth of today will never even get a glimpse of what those days were like. My sister and I tell our kids about those days all the time. That was before the fighting and the guns came into play. It was just fun. Point blank, growing up in Harlem was the shit. But even as a kid, I understood that Harlem was all about getting money, illegally of course, and I instantly got infatuated with that side of Harlem life. The truth is I got excited about the street life at an early age, but I would be lying if I said it was a life I had to indulge in to survive. That would be far from the truth. I grew up in a pretty good home, never wanting for nothing. Never feeling like I was poor. We always had food on the table. In fact, my mom usually cooked every day of the week. You see, my dad was Jamaican and loved to eat, so we had to have dinner five days a week when he was in town.

Hold up! They say everybody's life story starts with their parents and early childhood, so I guess I need to stop and take you back for a minute.

You see my mother was a Nurse. She's a southern girl, from Alabama. Ya'll know them southern girls from back then were built like stallions. She had a big ass and wide hips back in the day. Supposedly her and some handsome dude from Kingston, Jamaica bumped into each other on the train and became my parents. He saw those hips and that was it. LOL. My dad had businesses and a home back in Jamaica with a housekeeper and a cook. He was like a rich guy out there. He was one of the biggest poultry suppliers to major hotels and restaurants in Kingston. He also produced music and sold clothes and jewelry. That's a hustler for ya. He did well. Maybe that's where I got it from. But despite how successful he was, he always reminded me and my younger sister Shanda of his humble beginnings. He told us stories of how he had to walk miles to school with no shoes. I never forgot those stories, and even as a child I was more than grateful for all that GOD had blessed me with.

Anyway, dad went back and forth from New York to Jamaica a lot. He basically lived and handled his business in Jamaica while me, my mother and my sister lived in New York. He made a living exporting food, clothing, and jewelry from the States and selling it in Jamaica. I remember when he took us to Jamaica in 1986. My cousin Shelli came too. She was my best friend and we were inseparable back then. I'll never forget when we were driving to my dad's house from the airport. Shelli had a jeri curl at the time. The Jamaican kids surrounded the car like we were celebrities. My Pops told us that having a jeri curl was a luxury. It meant you had some money. That was the craziest shit I had ever heard. The kids were running along the road with the car asking us for money. My mother was in the front seat with her arm hanging out the window. She had on a thick 14 or 18 carat gold bracelet and my dad yelled at her to pull her arm back in the car before someone cut it off for that bracelet. I was like DAMN!!! Shit was rough for them out there.

If that wasn't crazy enough, when we got to the house, the housekeeper told us not to go off with anyone because we may never come back. She made one thing very clear: Jamaica can be a very dangerous place. Her name was Lynn and she cooked her ass off. It also didn't hurt that in addition to the ackee, ox tails and curry goat, she also made good American food. I was glad too because after seeing goats walking around or dead on the side of the road from being ran over, the last thing I wanted to do was sit down and eat one for dinner. My mother didn't care; she ate everything.

My dad was a real strict disciplinarian. He took education very seriously. He didn't play that being dumb shit. I use to have to stand in front of him and recite my time tables from 1 to 12. If I got to my 6 times tables and messed up, I had to start from 1 all over again. I grew up having to say "no daddy" "yes daddy" "no mommy" and "yes mommy." There was no just "no" or just "yes." My mother didn't care about all that stuff, but my father insisted it was a form of respect. If I forgot to answer properly, I got one of those real Jamaican ass whippings and slaps. That's when he was home in the States, of course. But like I've already said he spent a lot of time back home in Jamaica. His absence and my mom's overnights at the hospital gave me the freedom and opportunity I needed to explore the street life. You're probably wondering why I would risk being in the streets knowing the ass whippings I would get if my dad ever found out about it, right? Well, my curiosity about the streets always got the best of me. I just saw so much potential in the streets. I thought exploring those possibilities was worth it, and although I was scared to death of my dad, that fear didn't keep me away from the streets when he was gone.

I think the fashion aspect of the street life is what grabbed my attention too. At a very young age, I acquired an appreciation for fashion and dressing far beyond what my age dictated. In a way, I've always been exposed to some idea of style. My dad use to get a lot of his clothes tailor made, and my mom use to dress me really nice when I was a child, but when it comes to the style department my biggest influence was definitely my Aunt Myrtle. Although she grew up in Alabama with my mom, there wasn't nothing country about her except her accent. Myrtle worked in all the bars on 7th Avenue back in the days. There was the Night Cap, the Hucklebuck and Snookies. I use to think she owned Snookies because her nickname was Snookie. She was beautiful too. I mean that head turning kind of beauty, light skinned, freckles and a whole lot of sass. She messed with some real hustlers and players back in the day. Ya'll saw the movie American Gangster with Denzel, right? Well, we lived right down the block from Small's Paradise and Mr. B's. That's where all the players hung out in the 70's, and my Aunt knew them all. She was definitely that chick, and she dressed the part. I use to always wear her blouses, but I was too skinny to wear anything else of hers.

My Aunt Myrtle inspired me to understand that style is crucial, and by the time I got to Jr. high school me and Shelli were already rocking furs, nice jewelry, and sporting the latest pocketbooks. We wore names like Ellen Tracy, Adrienne Vittidini, Christian Lacroix, etc. back then. Shelli and I always had the latest pocketbooks. I think I was the only one in my school with an MCM briefcase. My boyfriend Stormin' Norman from St. Nick projects bought it for me back in '85. I see ya'll out there with ya'll bags today. I'm ahead of ya'll about what, 29 years. LOL. Norm was my first drug dealer boyfriend. I was around 16 at the time. He was doing his thing down in D.C and in Richmond Virginia. DC was murder capitol back then. There was a lot of money to be made in DC back then, which is probably why there were so many murders. They started calling it Murder Capital. Of course, as soon as dudes from New York heard about the potential to make money in DC, it was on. Ya'll already know. When we hear about that dough, we go crazy.

Shelli and I had a little crew of like ten chicks, but she and I did everything together. We're going to take a lot of those thing to our graves, so don't expect to read about it here. LOL. It's crazy when I think about the things we've done and the places we've been. Thinking back today, she and I agree that we put ourselves in some pretty dangerous situations that could have gone all wrong. We were chicks who loved the street life and the men in it.

We kept a dude with a couple of dollars. Well, a little more than a couple of dollars, but we were real low with who we dealt with. Not because it was a secret, but that's just how we were, plus we understood the game. Sometimes being quiet and on the low is better and safer, if you know what I mean. If you ask me, we got more out the deal moving the way we moved. We were young, but dudes knew we understood the way that street thing worked.

We were always going somewhere and doing something. We used to do shit like drive out of town just to go shopping or get our hair done. I remember this one time we drove out to DC for Howard University Home Coming and we stopped at this salon to get our hair done on some DC shit. OMG!!!! We got some crazy ass hairstyles. I can't remember the name of the salon, but YO!! The hairstyles were fly as hell for DC, but for Harlem, hell naw. We were crimped, primped, spritzed and looked like Halle Berry and that chubby chick in the movie BAPS. SMDH!!!! Can you imagine us coming back to Harlem with that shit on top of our heads? It was the funniest shit ever. We were just bored with a few dollars and just didn't know what to do with ourselves. But that's what that Harlem street life was all about, and that's what I fell in love with at such a young age.

R.I.P Zip, Troy, Keith (my dad), Aunt Myrtle

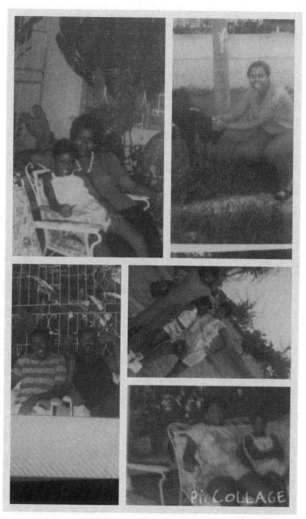

My mom, Lil Sis, Shelli and Pops in Jamaica

My Introduction
Into The Drug Game

Like I already said, I can't say that I was forced to engage in the street life. I can't say that my family was poor and hungry or that I did what I had to do to survive. That would all be lies. I turned to the streets because I was curious and I wanted more. Although my mom and dad were there and provided for me and my sisters, I still wanted more.

My quest into the street life began in '86. I started hustling on 123rd Street and 7th Ave. This is where I got my first lessons in the drug game. 123rd Street and 7th Ave was on FIRE! It seemed like that was where getting money began. It was just busy down there with so many people hanging out. My skinny ass was down there with my Louis Vuitton speedy bag full of angel dust. My product was called Dynamite. That shit had my bag smelling like spearmint gum. I hustled for my uncles, Wild Al and Big Stan, but I think it was Al that gave me the dust. I wasn't forced or anything like that. It's what I wanted to do. I was just too damn grown. Yeah, I remember it clear as day. It's crazy because I still can't believe I was in the middle of all that at such a young age. I was amongst big time drug legends. I know all about that brown paper bag and duffle bag money that those rappers be talking about. Not sure if they really know about it, but I guess it's nice to dream.

In '86, crack came through Harlem like a hurricane and overpowered the drug game. Well, it actually swept through the nation. L.A was hit hard too. There were killings and all kinds of shit going on because of crack. It was selling faster than heroin, dust, cocaine and weed combined. A lot of people had no clue how powerful crack really was or the long time effects it would have on them. Some bosses even started getting high off their own shit. Unfortunately, Wild Al happened to be one of them. Even though he got high, he was still a functioning boss. The fact that he was crazy as a motherfucker made it hard to tell if it was the crack or just him sometimes. LOL. He had Edgecombe on lock along with the Jamaicans. Al was the only American dude the Jamaicans allowed to hustle up there on the same block as them. There was no doubt he earned the "Wild" in Wild Al. He was one of a kind. I mean this dude use to have grenades in the house. I don't know if they were live or not, but the thought of him having them is insane. He used to bust people in the head with bottles for fun. He was crazy as a MF.

If a worker messed up any of Al's money, they knew it was a matter of life or death. He scarred people for life by beating them with different objects. Male or female felt the wrath of Al and his crack-high when they messed up. One day my girls and I were in the game room on 8th & 132nd Street and Shelli pulled some money out of his pocket. This fool pulled out a loaded gun and put it to her head. My sister Shanda flew out the game room and ran all the way home, which was only a block away, but it scared the shit out of her. My dude Butch told me a story about when him, Al and some other dudes were uptown and some chick walked by trying to be cute. They were all trying to holla, but she ignored them. Ole' girl learned a lesson that day. Butch said Al picked up a bucket of dirty ass water and threw it on the girl. Butch said he couldn't believe it. He said he told everybody to go get their gun because he knew that chick was coming back with somebody, but she didn't. That's just how crazy Al was. He just didn't give a fuck about nothing. He was funny as hell too. He would snap on you so hard til niggas wanted to cry because everybody else was laughing at them. When he was tired or bored, he sucked his thumb and then played with your ears. It sounds crazy, but it's true. I loved him to death. He drove us crazy sometimes, but we loved him and miss him dearly.

Stan was more laid back than Al, but he admired his older brother a lot. Stan was more of a mama's boy. I think Al had enough crazy for the both of them. Al had a lot of people scared of him, including his business partners. One business partner in particular, his so-called best friend Jacob, ended up setting him up to get killed, allegedly. It's said that Jacob had a dude named "Nile" that worked for them do the deed. It's crazy because both those dudes ate at my aunt's table. I learned early that you have to be very careful about who you break bread with. There is definitely no honor among thieves. Jacob was a smooth dude too. He was handsome, loved to dress and was getting money. He loved frontin' for the girls like all the street dudes did. I would've never guessed he would cross Al.

But the truth is Al had started acting crazy and wilding out on his own people. I can't say that Jacob didn't have a reason to do what he allegedly did, but I still hated him for it. The lesson I took from that situation was that the ones you have to watch out for are the ones that fear you the most. It's always the ones closest to you that sometimes mean you the most harm.

In a lot of ways Al got caught in a catch 22. You see, when you're in the street life, you need a right hand man. You need that person who can step up when you're not there. You need that person to handle business in your absence the same way you would if necessary. Somebody has to know the connect. Somebody has to know where the stash is. Unfortunately, for a lot of street dudes, that right hand man turned out to be their worst enemy. Either they were snitched on by them, or killed by them, which was the case with Al.

They got the drop on Al up on Edgecombe. He was wild all the way up to his death. He got shot four or five times with a .22 caliber, and was still talking shit.

"That punk got me," they say he said on the way to Harlem Hospital.

"Get these fucking bullets out of me," he shouted as they rolled him into the emergency room. But he never walked out that hospital. Apparently one of those bullets ricocheted through his body and hit some vital organs. He left the world the same way he came in, raising hell and talking shit. He died at the young age of 19.

The crazy thing is that Al was a teenager. My sister and I talk about that a lot. Nineteen years old then is definitely not nineteen years old today. He seemed so much older. We were so much more mature back then. Dudes were literally teenagers gettin' crazy amounts of money and handling their business. They were somebody's babies and to think, they were supporting whole families and neighborhoods.

Al's funeral was like a celebration. My aunt blasted "Fools Paradise," by Melisa Morgan in the funeral home at the viewing. A lot of people came through. The funeral was held at Metropolitan church, and guess who of all people sat behind me? Jacob. He was rocking and crying like he cared. I turned around and looked at him with disgust in my eyes.

"My aunt knows you're here?" I snapped.

"Yeah," he weakly replied.

I rolled my eyes and turned back around. I just wanted him to know that I knew he had something to do with it. I remember pulling my aunt aside later asking, "Why you let Jacob up in here?"

She looked at me with tears in her eyes and assured, "Baby don't worry about it. GOD will take care of everything."

I can't say I agreed with her position, but I respected her enough to accept it. The ride to the burial was like an out of town ride on Memorial Day. It was crazy. It was a real celebration of love. After Al died I stuck by Stan like glue. I started bottling up crack for him. My job was to make sure the block never ran out. That shit had my fingers sore as a MF. I was chopping day and night. Crack heads were going bananas over that crack shit. The way they were buying it, we couldn't chop fast enough. Crack was like ten and fifteen dollars. Later on somebody fucked the game up with duces and treys, two and three dollar cracks. Word on the street today is that the price went back up. I'm just saying, that's what I heard.

I eventually moved from bottling to collecting money off the blocks and paying the workers. Every night I gave the workers a little money after their shift and then paid them at the end of the week. I felt like a real boss. My uncle rounded up a crew of chicks to take my place bottling up the crack. I was happy with that promotion. Sometimes I chilled on the corner with the workers and watched them yell "Alice" or "One time" when a cop car came up the Ave. The police eventually figured out the workers were calling out warnings and harassed them whenever they caught them shouting those codes out.

I had the honor of going with Stan to re-up. Sometimes Stan paid for it and sometimes he got it on consignment. Getting drugs on consignment was a privilege. Everybody wasn't eligible for that deal. They didn't do that for everybody. But yo, making that re-up trip was a scary thing sometimes. We bought the drugs from up on Broadway. Broadway was cocaine capitol. All the connects were up there. Broadway was like little Columbia. Sometimes they were ready for us and brought the shit to our car when we got there, but sometimes we had to go up to one of their stash apartments. I hated when we had to go in. Every time we had to step foot in one of those apartments, it scared the shit out of me.

They answered the door holding big ass guns, and each time those doors shut behind us my heart dropped and then would beat so fast I thought it would jump out my chest. I always expected the worse. Sometimes Stan left me downstairs and I gave him a certain time to come back or I was calling the police. That's right motherfuckers I was snitching!!! LMAO. Every time we took a lot of money into one of those spots, it was a gamble with our lives. You just never knew if you were going to get burned. I didn't realize it then, but I put myself in so much danger just for a dollar.

Once we got the coke, we cooked it up, chopped it then flooded the block. That's how it went. And when we ran out we did it all over again.

I may have used a few terms in ways that some of ya'll readers are unfamiliar with, so let me take a minute to fill you in. If you don't know, re-up is when your supply of drugs is getting low and you make a purchase to meet the demand before it runs out. The connect is the person or people that supply drugs. And consignment is when you get the drugs free and pay later. I'm sure most of ya'll readers know what I'm talking about, but just in case some squares are reading, I have to help them keep up. LOL.

Since I didn't have to bottle up anymore I spent my time driving around frontin' and hanging out with my girls. We paid people to rent cars for us and rode around all day having fun. Stan had a friend named Andre that drove a black convertible corvette with red leather seats. Andre didn't think twice when I asked to hold it. He gave me the keys and that was it. I was riding around frontin' with the music blasting. That's how it all started. It's like once you got a taste of the fast life, there was no going back. It was like a high. You know you're doing something bad, but it's a rush because you're taking the risk. It was a game staying a step ahead of the police and getting a dollar more that the next man.

I thank Stan and Al for teaching me about the streets. No matter what one may think, without street smarts you know nothing. Street smarts are needed and can be used in any situation, even corporate America. That's why I don't understand why some of these dudes are still selling drugs today with no assets and no real business. I don't care how much money you got stashed, that shit don't mean anything. I don't care what kind of car you drive, it don't mean nothing. It's about owning shit these days. Back then owning a home or a business didn't really matter. The money was plentiful. But, today! Whatever you get, you better make it work for you.

It's so unbelievable to me that you dudes out here today don't even see your own potential. Selling drugs can be hard work. This is for those real hustlers that ran empires back in the day. If you can do that, you can do anything. If you have the smarts to weigh, count, divide and negotiate, you are a certified Accounting major with a concentration in Business. Fuck college!!!

Unfortunately, Stan is doing a FED bid for murder right now. He's been locked up since 1999 and hasn't been released as of this date. He took a plea because that's what real MEN do. He had no choice because snitches were on duty. He's short though. He'll be home soon. Hey Baldy ☐ .

R.I.P Wild Al, Kato, El, Joe

Big Stan

"This world doesn't have enough space to write the "LOVE" I have for you on. I am proud to be created at the same time and space-according to ALLAH (GOD) and to be sharing everything we've shared-especially the "LOVE"!!! What I carry inside for you, is eternal, and I really do not like to express these Strong-Feeling[s]-openly, because the world has changed since "OUR" beginning[s]... However, after the WORLD reads this memoir...the mindsight[s]may start to change back to the original way[s]of doing thing[s]!!! I have to tell you this now, because the world[s] watching "US"...

YOU TAUGHT ME "LOVE" WHEN I WASN'T EVEN OLD ENOUGH TO SPEAK OF LOVE-OUTSIDE OF MY MOTHER, AND BECAUSE OF[YOU] I KNOW EXACTLY HOW TO SEE A WOMAN-WHEN I WANT TO LOVE HER FOREVER!!! THANK YOU, FOR BEING MY FOREVER-FEMALE- MY NIECE, AND CONFIDANT-THE ONE(1) FEMALE-THE WORLD SAYS IS JUST-LIKE-ME!!!(WINK)... I LOVE YOU, AND CONGRATULATION[S]-YOU'RE ON YOUR WAY!!!;-)

YOUR UNCLE-MR.STANLEY "CHICKY"[DAVIS]

Wild Al

A Mr. Rob exclusive, LOL. '80 something

There's Levels to This Shit

All the little youngsters coming up wanted to be the next Rich Porter, Alpo or AZ. The AZ's and Rich Porters wanted to be like the older more seasoned street hustlers like Fritz, who was once known as the richest man in Harlem, aka the Consignment King, and others. Fritz was the best that ever did it; at least one of the best. All the dudes wanted his kind of money. These guys were doing their thing and made a name for themselves in the streets of Harlem. They were the role models that were looked up to. They were the street entrepreneurs of their day. The young dudes studied the way they did business and how the ladies gravitated to them, willing to do anything just to be in their presence. They had a swagger that some tried to imitate. Unfortunately, tragedy struck many of these men like it did my uncle Al. Unimaginable things happened because of jealousy and envy. I guess that's the risk they took to get to that level of street royalty. The real tragedy of the street life is that most of the time it's the people closest to you that cause you the most pain.

Risk and pain aside, the drug game was addicting. The flashy cars and jewels were enticing, especially for the ladies. That's what the ladies loved. If you were a man, that's why your girl left you to be with the next man. If you were a woman, that's why your man left you to be with the next bad bitch. No matter what a dude looked like, if he had cash he was guaranteed to get any bitch he wanted. That "he's fine" shit didn't mean anything. If a dude went from ugly and broke to "that nigga with all that money," he just went from ugly to "he's alright" and maybe even cute. That cash flow is all that mattered.

For dudes getting money, there was always a wifey and a side chick or two. Everybody had to play their position. Wifey drove the cars, stayed at the crib, spent her day shopping, and was introduced to only close friends. A lot of times the wifey had to stay in. She didn't come out too much. Now although the side chick had to meet her man at the hotel and couldn't get as much time with him, she came off pretty good too. The side chick was everywhere. She was allowed to run the streets. All the homeys knew the side chick, and after the hotel she was hit off with a gang of cash. Don't sound like a bad deal to me. In fact, sometimes you never knew that a wifey existed because she was seldom seen, and that was how her man wanted it.

"You don't need to be out like that, dudes might try to snatch you to get me," wifey's man often told her.
Mmmm hmm. Yeah ok. That's the bullshit they ran. Personally nobody could've ever said that to me. I was never a good listener anyway.

The wifey sometimes accepted the other chick being with her man. Shit, to be honest some of them still do. SMH!!!! Ya'll know who ya'll are. They either dealt with it or gave it all up. Most chose to ignore the fact that the other woman even existed. Every now and then, the wifey saw the side chick here and there at parties or whatever with an outfit on that her man most likely paid for. She would snicker in a corner with her girlfriends all the while wondering, "Why? How could he cheat on me with that!" Sometimes a fight broke out, and guess what? They both still stayed with the motherfucker. Yep that's just how it went. Sometimes it wasn't worth the headache to be the wifey. It was better to just get the money and enjoy the moment.

Dudes got a kick out of having their cake and eating it too. Sometimes it went too far. Sometimes a dude with the money attempted to have the next dude's chick from another crew. That caused bloodshed. With that said, please listen carefully. There are two things street dudes need not to do:

1) fuck with another man's money; and 2) fuck with another man's main chick. Pussy was definitely the reason for a lot of beef in the streets. But it was all about the dough. If a dude in the crew started getting too much money, his status and the amount of pussy he got went up, but so did the amount of envy amongst his closest friends. And that envy caused those friends to make moves.

The most common of all street moves was attempting to

move up from worker to boss status. Basically, this was when an ambitious worker rounded up his own crew of workers, made up of lil thirsty dudes eager to be a part of the life, and tried to make deals with the connect behind his boss' back. Those were some risky moves. I guess wanting the money outweighed the risk, and many thought taking the risk was worth it in order to get to a higher level in the game.

That was the hood back then. There were rules to be followed. You either respected the code of the street or got dealt with. At the end of the day, power respects power, so none of that other shit mattered. When two dudes with power in the streets had a problem with each other, and both were about their business, they could settle the problem without ever speaking a single word. The respect was automatically given and everybody understood what was and wasn't going to be tolerated.

Some people that I mention in this book put a lot of time and effort into their craft. Their skill was selling large amounts of cocaine at a fast rate in order to make more money than the next guy. There will never be anyone like them. They were in a class by themselves. Anybody can sell drugs, but some individuals had a uniqueness about them. It could have been their looks, their character or the way they walked. It could have been anything that made them stand out more than the others. Each was special in his or her own way. Oh, let me be clear there were some real boss chicks on the scene that were getting' money back then too. Not to glorify anything that they did, but they wouldn't be the street legends they are if there wasn't people like us who looked up to them and admired them for who they were. It's now 15, 20 and 25 years later and you still hear their names being mentioned. Rappers shout them out in their songs. Movies and documentaries have been made about them. These street legends appear on magazine covers. They were Harlem. Some have been gone for a while now, but they will never be forgotten. Some are memorialized every year with block parties that are packed from one avenue to another.

These guys got to street levels that some dudes only dreamed about. I'm happy to have been a part of that era. It was a time I will always remember. Although it was a fun time, the same question comes up over and over again. Was it all worth it? Was the risk worth the reward? Back then it was. This brings me to a very important point. A lot of people took those risks, but not everyone got the same reward. Some did it better than others and in different ways. They might have looked like they were doing the same thing, but they weren't. You see, there's a difference between a hustler and hustling. A real hustler could rob you and sell you your own shit back. You know it's yours, but his delivery is so smooth that he makes you second guess yourself. A real hustler is good at his craft. A hustler is going to make money regardless of his circumstances. So even though there were a lot of people hustling back then, not everyone was a true hustler.

A hustler is anybody that can stand on any street corner and sell a product, make a profit and do it all over again and again, day after day, using that money to make more money. The product doesn't have to be drugs. People hustle every day. That Lil Mexican woman that comes out on that corner everyday in the summer selling slices of oranges and mangos is a hustler. If you work a nine to five and you're sitting at that office desk and already know how you're gonna flip that check so you can make more money, you're a hustler. But you have to know that there are levels to this shit. Being a boss is not for everybody. Some are made to be bosses and some are made to just be employees. Just because you see a dude on the corner day in and day out selling drugs doesn't mean he's a hustler. Most likely he's just wasting his goddamn time. He's probably that bum ass dude that sells drugs just to have enough money to buy weed, get high and take a chick to a hotel. I'm sure he stays broke, lives with his mama and has kids he doesn't take care of. The sad shit is that he's content with that. He's just hustling. He's not a hustler. I'm just saying. There's a different breed of hustlers today. They're nothing like the hustlers of yesterday.

I was there for those Harlem street legends, and I also had the honor of knowing one lil dude that was determined to get to that boss level one day too. He was young and he was going to get the respect he wanted from the streets. More than that, he was gonna replace those fallen soldiers that preceded him. He was gonna do it bigger and better. Everybody was gonna one day know who he was and it wasn't going to be easy to forget him. He was determined to change the game. He was going to do it big, more than that he was going to do it his way.

To know him was to love him. He was handsome, funny as hell and had the cutest smile. He wasn't a very serious person except when it came to taking care of business. Even then he was cool. He loved his family and his crew. He took care of his family as well as his crew. His charm is what drew the girls to him. His swagger is what made the fellas want to be like him. He wanted the cars, the jewelry, the money and the women. He was determined to get to those levels.

He wanted to be like Rich Porter and get the money. He wanted to be like Lou Sims and get the respect. Later in his years, he reminded me of Fritz. He loved to give. When he later became the man in the streets, all the dudes wanted a piece of the action, his action. He was about getting his money, and if you wanted a chance to get some, he gave you that chance. He even gave his haters a chance. It fueled his ego to do so. Those who had been standing on street corners for years envied what he accomplished in a mere year and a half. They needed what he had. They wanted his life, even if it meant trying to take it from him.

Whether they called him Jermaine, Maine, or Baby Jay, that day would come when you knew who they were referring to. Whether people wanted to or not, they were gonna one day know who he was.

Who was Maine, aka Baby Jay? He was a father, a son, a brother, and a friend. He was also **A MADE NIGGA.**

Baby Jay:
When We Met Maine

Maine came into my life when he was about fifteen years old. It was a summer night in 1987 and my girls and I were doing our usual thing, sitting on the hood of a car in front of my building on 8th Avenue. Everybody was out. People were walking and driving up and down the Avenue. My sister Shanda was about twelve years old at the time. She was always with me. Although we were six years apart, we were always together. I took her everywhere. It wasn't like other sibling relationships. Our father raised us to love each other. Fighting with each other was a no no. I loved having her with me. I taught and she followed my lead. Thank GOD she didn't follow everything. Wooooo!!!!

Anyway, that night Lil Sis came up to me and said "Tee, this boy wants to take me out to eat."

I looked at my girls, turned back to my sister laughing and said, "Who?"

"His name is Jermaine," she answered.

"Where he wanna take you?" I asked

"That steak house called Flaming Embers."

I was thrown back a bit because that was the spot. I knew she was talking about the steak house on 86th Street, on the East Side. That was one of the spots that everybody went to. It was one of the spots where the hustlers liked to eat at. Shit, my nigga took me there, and there my sister was at twelve with somebody wanting to take her there. I had to know who this Jermaine kid was.

"I need to meet him first," I said.

He walked up a few minutes later. I didn't know he was right across the street the whole time with four of his boys watching my reaction while she asked me for permission to go. He was a little cutie, a handsome little thing, skinny with a cute smile. He was nicely dressed, very respectful and somewhat shy.

"Hey, how you doing?" he greeted with the biggest and cutest smile I had ever seen. "Can I take Shanda out to eat?"

Although I already knew the answer, I asked, "Where?"

He answered, but I was too busy staring at him and my sister standing side by side. I thought that was the cutest thing. I was like a proud mother seeing her child go on a first date. They made a cute couple.

"Look at my baby," I thought.

Her hair was in braids with colored rubber bands on the ends, and she had on a blue and white cheerleader skirt. He had on a white t-shirt and blue jeans. His jeans kind of sagged, but not because they were into sagging back then. He was just skinny and didn't have enough ass to hold them up. I remember it like it was yesterday.

"How old are you?" I asked him.

"Fifteen."

He was a teenager, but that didn't bother me because I knew Lil Sis knew how to conduct herself and not be taken advantage of. Plus, she was a fighter. Most likely if he tried anything she would have whipped his ass. Fo' real. LOL.

Before they left I pulled her to the side. "Dinner don't mean touching, kissing or anything else. And when you're done, you say thank you and let him bring you home."

I wasn't letting Lil Sis get used by no one. Giving up the goods for food was a no no. But of course there were some chicks fucking up the game by doing that shit. They had the game twisted and messing it up for everybody else. Once a chick did that, dudes thought all chicks were down for giving it up to eat. It also lessened the respect dudes had for chicks. Sometimes it worked out for chicks for much more than dinner, because pussy is a powerful thing. Today some men still think that if they take you to dinner you got to fuck. It's sad because some chicks still think that's the way to play the game. But then again, a lot of women are the bread winners today, so some of us don't really need dudes like that. We're buying dinner these days.

Lil sis was a little cutie with a cute body so I had to make sure she understood what she was worth. At that time I had mastered boys and men. I knew what to do and how to do it. I learned the power of pussy at a young age. I was game tight and I was gonna make sure nobody was going to take advantage of her.

I know you're thinking, "How could you let her go on a date at 12?" Like I said before, back then it was different. She knew how to respect herself. She knew how to take care of herself.

While they waved a cab down his little crew across the street waved at him and walked off laughing and slapping each other five like little boys do. They were all too cute.

Maine was from 5th Avenue, Lincoln Projects. I had never been over there. I never had a reason to go. The East Side and the West Side kinda did their own thing. They did their thing and we did ours, but there was no beef.

After that night, I would go with Sis over to the East side and Maine and his friends would come to our house and chill. It was crazy being around them. It was like five or six of them. Maine was like the ring leader. They were true to what they were living in those streets. They were young, but they were the truth. It was Maine, Dee, Gee, Roc, Spanish Babote, Lil Eric, and Mike Murder. Mike Murder and Lil Eric are actually the older brothers of Max B, who eventually became one of the best rappers out, but Max B was young and home with his mom back then.

Maine and Mike Murder came under their older cousins Boogie and Hector who ran with a Spanish dude named Daddy. They were all gettin' money. Hector was like a father to them. They admired him a lot. He showed them how to get money and conduct themselves like businessmen. Hector was a real smooth dude. He was reserved and laid back. He hustled out in D.C sometimes too, where he and Daddy eventually would be killed in separate incidents. Maine and Mike really took their deaths hard. They were the closest to them. Maine wanted to be like them and he was going to make sure he and his crew got to that level.

Maine and his crew were like little masters of the hustle game. He and his little crew were the funniest little people I ever met. Maine and his man Gee were the brains of the operation and the rest were like little soldiers who were ready to set it off at any given time. When it came to the streets, they all pretty much went with the flow of whatever Maine and Gee did. Gee was real quiet and mysterious. He was actually a year or two older than Maine. He looked like he was always thinking. He didn't act young like the rest of them.

It was crazy because Maine and his crew were hustling at the young ages of fourteen, fifteen and sixteen years old. They were back and forth mainly between N.Y and D.C. Murder ended up getting arrested and sentenced to do some time. The unsettling thing for me is that Murder and Maine would end up doing bids upstate and never being on the street at the same time again. Whenever one came out, the other had already gone in. They couldn't wait to be on the streets together again. I mean, they saw each other on visits, but that street reunion never happened.

They hung out at my house a lot. My mom was always working the night shift and my dad of course was in Jamaica, so we pretty much had the house to ourselves. I let Maine and his crew spend the night at my house all the time, to keep them off the streets. They would be knocked out all over the place. Roc's crazy ass always pulled the sofa away from the wall and slept behind it next to the radiator. He said he liked to sleep on the part of the carpet that wasn't walked on. I always woke them up at about 6:30 am so they could be out by the time my mom got home at 7:00 am. That was our routine. There was nothing I wouldn't do for them. If Maine needed to stash something at my house it was no problem, but he rarely did that. That's how it was.

One time the police and warrant squad came banging on the door early in the morning looking for Maine, but he wasn't there. Stan happened to be outside that morning holding his corner down. He said they had the building surrounded waiting for Maine's lil ass to run out. LMAO! That's because whenever he got locked up he would use my address and called me first. He could've called his mother, but I know he didn't want to worry her.

It was fun having them around. They were hilarious. I remember when Dee and Lil Eric made up a dance off that song "The Symphony" by the Juice Crew with Kool G Rap. It was the funniest shit I ever seen. They were like little comedic gangstas. They would make up dances and joke around, just being kids, yet they were running the streets hustling and taking care of business like men. Despite all of that they were good kids. They were just a product of their environment. They were curious just like I had been.

Maine looked out for Lil sis. By the time school started everyone knew who her boyfriend was. She had just started Junior High School, and he would pick her up for lunch and took her and her friends out to eat every afternoon. And if he and his crew were going out of town for a few days, he made sure she had money. Whenever they returned, they made sure we were alright. We were like family. I remember my sister telling me that a teacher pulled her aside at school one day.

"Are you okay?" The teacher asked. "We hear you're messing with a drug dealer."

They asked her that in Junior High School. LMAO. That was crazy. It's obvious that his presence was definitely known. I'm not condoning little twelve year olds messing with street dudes, especially now a days. The kids today are different. Their maturity level is different.

I loved Maine, he was my heart. He is my heart. I know people use to wonder what it was about him that made me protective of him. He was loyal and made sure his people was alright. He treated me with the utmost respect. If we had any issues in the streets, he held us down. He was not your ordinary little dude. I respected his hustle. The streets respected his gangsta. There weren't too many fifteen year olds that could hustle and had the street smarts like he did.

Fifteen year olds today are nowhere near as street smart or mature as the fifteen year olds of yesterday. The mentality of these kids today is different. They are straight knuckleheads. These kids today are running around in the streets with guns shooting people for no reason. The sad part is that half of them are punks and are in gangs because they aren't bad enough to stand alone. I'm not saying that it was right to shoot anybody back then, but it wasn't as reckless as it is today.

Most of the recklessness has to do with parenting. Some parents are only 15 years older than their kids and still want to hang out with, smoke weed with and party with their kids. The shit is crazy. Not to mention that far too many black men are not present in their kids' lives. And GOD knows we need black fathers to be a part or their children's lives. The absence of these black fathers has resulted in their children having a lack of respect for everybody.

Was Maine an angel? No he wasn't, but he wasn't robbing and stealing from nobody. He made his own lane and walked in it. I never condoned any reckless behavior, and there were occasions when Maine and his boys did something reckless. At times they needed guidance, and they were respectful enough to listen to the voices of reason that were Boogie, Hector and when necessary me.

R.I.P Hector, Daddy, Babote, Lil Eric

Me, Mike Murder, Shanda and Maine

1987

It was summer, a year after Al died, and we had his first memorial service in the school yard across the street from my building. At the time I was in a relationship with a lil dude named Cal. He was young, wild and from Brooklyn, but he and his family had moved to Harlem. Cal was a lil hustling MF. Although he was young, he ran with older guys. Him and Stan's friend Jamie-O were tight. I actually witnessed Jamie-O put in work on the streets. He was definitely not to be played with. Jamie-O was like a big brother to him. Unfortunately, Cal was forced to take care of himself at a young age. He had family, but the streets were his family. Thinking back on Cal's situation makes me realize that sometimes we have to stop and thank GOD for what we have and for our families. Sometimes we don't realize what others had to do and what some kids still have to do to survive. We forget that we can't pick our families and how we're raised. So if you had a good family upbringing, thank GOD for that. That's what I learned from Cal's situation. Witnessing his struggle at such a young age made me appreciate the little things in life a lot more.

At the time I was still hustling for Stan and doing me. Stan was always trying to school me on the streets and how to do business. He and I rode around all day listening to the Ojays' "Stairway to Heaven" and "Loving You." We also listened to a lot of Frankie Beverly and Maze, Teddy P and all that good shit. I had an early appreciation for the oldies. I even got Cal hooked on that shit. Cal and I use to be in my house having sex off of "Living Together in Sin" by the Whispers and "How Deep is Your Love" by Keith Sweat. SMH!!! That was some crazy shit. We were like seventeen and eighteen years old. We were just too damn grown.

That summer, just a few months after Cal and I got together,

I found out that I was pregnant. I was happy, but sick as a dog. Cal was excited. But the happiness was short lived. I had a miscarriage almost right after I found out about the pregnancy. We were both sad about it, but things happen for a reason. We loved each other, but we fought over little stuff all the time. I remember one night he went crazy on me over a phone call from some fool I didn't even know claiming he paid someone for my number. Cal was on the living room phone line and I was on the kitchen phone line and we were looking at each other while this guy told that lame ass story. As bad as I wanted to hang up, I wanted that conversation on the phone to last forever because the look in Cal's eyes told me that all HELL was going to break loose in that house after we hung up. And it did. Cal commenced to hitting on me and just going crazy. I still can't believe that dude said he paid someone for my number and I never found out who he was. That was some crazy and desperate shit to say. It wasn't like I was one of those chicks that was even out there like that. WTF!!!!!

I loved Cal, but at the time we both were young and not really as committed to being in a serious relationship. He was doing his thing and I just wasn't in the position where I even cared.

The night of Al's memorial, Cal and I were on the corner talking when one of Stan's high school friends came through in a red convertible BMW. He looked at me, I looked at him, and that was the beginning of something new. Yo, I was a mess ya'll. LMAO. His name was Dog. He was from Manhattan Avenue. He and his partner Kev Frost were both young and gettin' a gang of cash. Kev was only 15 when I met them and their money was long. So, ya'll already know. A bitch was like, "What Up?" I played it cool though because this MF Stan was a nut and then there was Cal who was running around doing him. Did he think I didn't know? He thought wrong. But we hadn't officially broken up yet, plus I had just lost the baby.

If the name Frost sounds familiar that's because Kev Frost is the younger brother of a reality star. Kev was a cutie and had all the older chicks on lock. Cute plus an asshole full of money equals you get all the bitches.

Stan started going down to Manhattan Ave and would take me with him. He noticed the way Dog and I looked at each other, and he didn't approve of that shit at all. "Stay away from my niece,"

39

he tried to threaten Dog, but it was too late for all that shit Stan was talking about. Dog and I started calling each other and talking on the low, and we hit it off rather quickly. He had a girl at the time. She lived on his block. He already knew what he had to do about that. He cut her off and it was just me and him. But before all that happened I broke it off with Cal. It was headed that way anyway. He came to the house to get his things, but before I let him in, I called security to come upstairs just in case he got crazy. That didn't work. On the way out the apartment, he punched me right in my fuckin' eye. Security didn't do shit. A little bubble formed right in the corner of my eye. But shit, if that's all it took for me to be with Dog, I had to charge it to the game.

For many nights, Kev and Stan wondered where the hell Dog started disappearing to late at night all of a sudden. They never thought to drive down my block until one night they saw his car parked in front of my building. He had been coming to see me for a few weeks and they never even knew or suspected it. Stan was heated, but what could he do.

Unfortunately, Dog had a case pending and ended up getting five years in the FEDS. He was my first boyfriend that went to jail, I think. I was 18 and really didn't know how to deal with that. My plan was to wait for him. I visited him up in Otisville Federal facility a few times. It was cool and all until he ended up in Indiana, which ruled out visiting as an option. All that time and distance eventually came between us and gave way for me to indulge in other relationships.

Unfortunately, Cal ended up in jail too. I was like DAMN!!!!! We weren't together at the time, but I was still sad to hear what happened. He ended up blowing trial for a lot of years. I visited him a few times too up until the early nineties and then the visits stopped, but I stayed in touch with his family over the years.

R.I.P Jamie-O, Alimo (119th St)

Very Unique

T hat same summer of 1987, Stan had bought a red Chevy Blazer and put me in it and kept money in my pocket. I guess he did it so I wouldn't ride with dudes or have to ask dudes for anything. I remember sitting in the car in front of Willie Burgers one night with this dude from downtown. He was tall with some big ass feet. He was leaning back in the front seat with his foot on the dashboard. The next thing I knew a big ass ashy hand came through the passenger window and knocked my friend's foot off the dashboard.

"Motherfucker, get your feet off my dashboard," Stan barked. "Bitch get this nigga out my car."

He scared the shit out of us. I was like this MF is crazy. Stan cock blocked like crazy. He was always threatening dudes to stay away from me. It didn't work though. I did what I wanted to do. I guess he knew how he treated chicks and didn't want me being treated like that, but he didn't know that I knew how to run game on MF's. He really had nothing to worry about.

It was around this time that I met Unique. If you're from Harlem I'm sure you've heard of him. If you don't know him or never heard of him, he's the one that came up with and started that "Aaaayoo, Aiightt" call and response that be getting the parties jumping. Yeah, he came up with that, not Dougie Fresh, not Naughty by Nature, it was Unique. Anyway, the name Unique suited him well because he was definitely one of a kind.

One day I was on the elevator in my building when this guy got on and said, "You're a pretty black bitch."

I was stunned to say the least. I snapped like, "Who are you talking to?"

"Nah ma, I don't mean to be disrespectful, but you're a pretty black bitch," he attempted to smoothly explain.

"I'm not a bitch."

I didn't mind the black part because my ex-boyfriend Norm gave me the name Black back in '85, and had been calling me that ever since. Ya'll might be thinking WTF was up with dude. Exactly! But believe it or not there was something about this dude that was intriguing. I started seeing him coming and going more and more. He was always dressed real nice and drove nice cars. He invited me up to his apartment one day, but I realized he shared the apartment with a chick and was like, "Nah, I'm good."

Now, I'm sure you're like, "Damn, this bitch jumped from one MF to the next." But not really. I was young and engaged to "the life", not those MF's. Not to mention the last two just got locked up. We good now?

Back to Unique. He had a style about him that was very attractive. Remember back to when I spoke about "being cute vs. having money." This is what I meant. Unique wasn't one of those fine ass brothers in the traditional sense. He wasn't light skin with curly hair, not that I ever cared for that type anyway. He had charisma. He was good looking, charming and had a beautiful smile. He treated you good and he had the money to do it. He was very confident, dressed well, and had a nice jewelry collection too. He was loud, and I mean LOUD, very energetic and always made his presence known wherever he went. It was like once he entered your life he was there to stay. That's partly because some didn't want him to leave. I became one of those women that couldn't get enough of being in his presence.

We kept talking here and there. I guess he wanted more than just talking so out of respect he moved around the corner and into his own apartment, which I came to visit from time to time. We kind of just became a couple. Well, I'm sure I was one of a couple of girls he dealt with. Not willingly of course. In my Jamaican accent, "Mi nah play dat shit"!!! LOL

Unique and my family became tight. He, my mom, Aunt Myrtle and Lil Sis were cool. He especially liked Lil Sis. She was like the little sister he never had. He took her everywhere he went. Every time he got a new car he called her and took her for a ride. One day he tried to teach her how to drive and she wrecked the car by running into a construction site. He told her to back up and they got the fuck up out of their quickly. He just bought another car. He loved her and gave her anything she needed. One time when he and I had a fight, he flew out to Virginia for a day and took Shanda with him. I guess he called himself punishing me by leaving me in NY. He later had a baby by a chick out there, so I guess that's what he was really up to out there. Slick MF. LOL.

He loved to party and loved women even more. He was Jamaican, but very much Americanized. He loved to get high. He was high all day and all night. He woke up lighting blunts. He told me that he was more alert and aware of his surroundings when he was high. Speaking of awareness, Unique and Stan are the reason I don't place my trust in many people. They taught me to be on point. They taught me to be on point about someone following me home and things like that. I remember Stan use to cross the George Washington to Jersey just to turn around and go home to the Bronx or wherever else he was staying at the time just to make sure he wasn't being followed. He also taught me that whenever I crossed a bridge to always get a receipt. You never know when the police were going to accuse you of being somewhere you weren't, and with the way the justice system always hated on black men, it made a lot of sense. And it still does. Not to mention that snitches were always on duty ready to blame you for anything to free their own asses and that's still the case today.

Unique was definitely taking care of business in the streets. The first time I ever saw a money machine was at his house. He always had some new tricked out car. Those were the days when everybody had their car piped out. You had to have leather seats to have piping. Unique had the white Benz with white seats and mint green leather piping. It may have been the other way around, but that motherfucker was pretty. Carlos from the Auto Clinic up on Jerome Avenue was making a gang of cash doing that. Then there was the hidden stash boxes in the cars. Shout out to Gadget Mike. My dude ended of doing decades for that shit. Can ya'll believe that shit? Decades for making stash boxes. He's still in. The snitches got him too.

Unique's jewelry game was tight too. One day when we were at his house he showed me a large Ziplock bag full of jewelry that he didn't wear. He told me that I should always by jewelry that was worth something because if times got hard I could pawn it and start over. I thank him for that because those hard days definitely came. His jewelry was his money bag in case shit ever got thick.

Unique attracted men and women. They were attracted to his lifestyle and his rambunctious personality. The dudes wanted to know who he was and where he came from. They wanted to get the money and the women like he did. A lot of dudes were jealous because he was different. The women just wanted to be with him. He was somewhat intoxicating. It was something about him that made you want to be in his presence. I found myself wanting to always be around him, but he made me crazy at times. It was a crazy relationship with me and him though. It was fun because being around him was like a 24-hour party.

Unique ended up moving to another apartment on 151st and 8th Avenue. He also rented the store front of the building that was a studio, a weed spot and a record store all in one. It was called Mecca Audio. He and I got into many fights over his constant flirting and messing around with other chicks. For a lot of women, getting high with Unique for free was enough for them to get fucked. It bugged me out how they settled for so little just to be around him. I didn't get high so that didn't matter to me. But I will tell you this; the brother is extremely blessed, if you know what I mean. That didn't matter to me either. I never allowed dick to make me stupid.

I remember one year we all went to Bear Mountain Park and WILD OUT! It seemed like it was about a hundred of us. We were walking around with Unique leading the way with his loud ass singing a record made in his studio. Me, Shelli, Shanda and his boy Bigga was on the track. Ya'll gotta picture this shit. Can you imagine a bunch of black people walking around the park in our bikinis and swimsuits, with the guys singing, "I like to get my alright now sucked, sucked." "I like to get my alright now sucked, sucked." Those white folks frantically snatched their kids, covering their eyes and ears in shock. They didn't understand what the fuck was going on. Looking back, I know they called us all kinds of negroes that day. You really had to be there, but if you know Unique you already know how it went down. WHEREVER this dude was it was a party. We could just be standing on the block and he'd make it a party.

We use to go to the Ebony Lounge that was on 5th Avenue

and turn up. We really had a ball. Me and one of my so-called friends from the Bronx almost got into it in there because that freak bitch was really playing Unique close. I'm sure she had sex with him. Her name's not worth mentioning. It's hilarious to me that chicks think they're doing something by sexing your man. They think that they're gonna get what you get, but eight times out of ten it's not the case. Honey you're just going to get fucked and sent home with a wet ass. It's not worth degrading yourself as a woman. All you're going to do is lose your friends and get labeled as a freak. Some chicks really didn't care about that back then and still don't. They didn't care if they were labeled a freak. I've never been a trifling type of chick. I always had my own man. I always knew my worth and getting fucked for sport wasn't in my play book. This was never free. Don't get me wrong, I wasn't selling pussy, but it wasn't free. There were times when I got with someone that I was attracted to and it was on. Then there were times when they came after it, wanted it bad, and were willing to do anything to get it. That's just the way it was.

Unique was who he was and I had to take him as he was or leave his ass. He had apartments all over the place. One day I went to his apartment in the Bronx on Field Place. I knew he was there because his jeep was parked outside, but he wouldn't answer the door. Of course he was there with another chick, so I decided to add air conditioning to his jeep by breaking all the windows. Yeah I was a crazy MF. It was an ivory colored Montero. The funny thing was that he wasn't even mad.

"Black is crazy," was his only response. Can ya'll believe that shit?

I think that pissed me off more. I was very jealous when I was with him. Good pussy would make a nigga crazy, but good dick mixed with a lot of money, sprinkled with a crowd of chicks wanting your man will make a bitch lose her mind too. LOL.

But I had made a vow to myself that after Norm I would never let another man stress me out. Chicks flocked around Unique like little puppies and I refused to be one of them. No matter what, he always showed me love, but I had to step away from our relationship. But even after we stopped messing around, the respect, love and friendship was still there between us. And it's no different today.

45

Street Image

Image was always important in the streets of Harlem.

Either you were "that nigga" in the streets or you weren't. There was no faking it. If you were tested, you had to show and prove. When it came to hustling you either worked for the money or let the money work for you. You always knew who was holding. Meaning, you could tell who was really making money and who was just getting by, frontin'. You knew who the boss was and who the worker was. The worker was always the one trying extra hard to be noticed.

From a young kid to the day he died, Maine was a hustler. He made money and was determined to always do it big. He never changed. He was who he was. His status eventually changed, but he was always Maine. His ego grew a little bigger, but he was still that dude that would give you whatever you asked for.

In Harlem everybody wanted to be somebody. If you were that dude acting like you were getting money, trust me there was a chick that was about her business that was gonna scheme to get you. If you were a dude that portrayed to be thorough, then trust there was a dude that was waiting to test you.

Rich Porter was "That dude." He was that dude that got paper and flossed heavy. He could do that. He was a hustler, a drug dealer and a master at his craft. He was that dude the chicks wanted. He was also that dude that others wanted to be like or scheme on.

Fritz was "The Man." He was the one that could make you a Rich Porter. He created bosses in the streets of Harlem. He never portrayed to be a gangster or a murderer, and the two should never be mixed anyway. As rich as he was, he never flaunted it. He did his thing and he did it well. He was well respected for it. If you met him in the streets you would have never known you were talking to a rich guy. He was a cool guy and I liked his style. He wasn't flamboyant. He wasn't arrogant. He never tried to play you. He just did him. He never looked to be validated. If you're gonna go out, do it like they did. That's the way it should be, with people admiring you and speaking your name decades after you're gone, but with grace.

It wasn't always about being a hustler, a gangster or a murderer back then. I guess it's the same thing today. If you choose to portray that image in the streets, you need to be prepared for what comes with it. Like some entertainers for instance, they have names like Killa This, Gangsta That or Murder Somethin'. But we know they've never killed anyone or anything. But I'm sure there's a knuckle head out there waiting to test them. Not because they did anything to him, but because their names alone suggest that they're bragging about being tough or about that street life. It's funny because I ran through the streets of Harlem all my life and I've never heard or seen some of these rappers anywhere before a certain period of time. Not even at a party. I hear them on TV and radio screaming out the names of street legends they probably didn't even know in real life. I listen to them acting hard, like they're about the life, but I know the truth.

A couple of years ago my ex, Lou called and asked who this one rapper was that was acting like he ran Harlem? I won't say who he was asking about, but we just laughed because these rappers know not what they do. Some even go as far as claiming to be big time drug dealers, but hey, we all can dream. The beauty of the rap game is that it's all about entertainment and fantasizing anyway, right? Whether these rappers mean to seem like gangsters or not, that's how it's perceived. Whether these street guys want to portray the gangster life or not, that is how it is perceived. "DIP" who? LOL

Before I go on, let me make something clear, one person or one group does not represent the entire Harlem. They do not speak for everybody. I see a lot of cornball shit going on and I'm not feeling it. I've heard stories of some who use to get played in the streets, but I'm not going to call him out. Then they grow up talking about they run Harlem and did this and that, but yet I never saw or heard of them. They walk around talking about they knew Rich or this one or that one. If you did okay, but if you didn't that's okay too. Just be you. I be listening to cats talk and just shake my head.

Don't get me wrong, I love Harlem and our time has come again for us to get money on all levels. We're about to do it again, but the right way this time. I just can't take all that extra shit. My point is this. Whoever you were or whoever you are it's okay to be just that. And for the record, those folks from "Black Ink" DEFINITELY don't rep for Harlem. I don't know who the hell they are. SMMFH!

Lou Sims was a person who may have tested those perceptions and checked some of these dudes' tough skills. He was somewhat of a street legend and magnificent at his craft, so they say. He sounds like a poet or an artist, but according to the press he was one of the most dangerous men that ever ran the streets of Harlem. Still, to me he was sweet, funny, and charming. To others he was scary, mean, a gangster and a murderer.

He had Harlem in an uproar. Just the mention of his name had dudes almost shitting their pants. Was it because he did something to them? Was it because they actually saw his work? Or was it that they just took the word of the streets and ran with it? Did Lou portray this image or was it just who he was? Once one person says something and it spreads, it's hard to get rid of it. It doesn't even matter if it's all rumors and false allegations. And since I brought up rumors and allegations, let me tell you that there are two things that can arise from a negative street image. Those two things are death and a bid in Prison.

But let me get back to Lou. Regardless of what they say about him or what he did, he will always be the realest dude I know. He's a stand up guy. He's a guy who took thirty years without hesitation. He did this when most of his so-called comrades decided to snitch on him. Only a few of his people took their time like men. Lou is still serving his thirty year sentence standing up and fighting against what those snitches and rats said he did. He never once thought about telling on anyone.

A few years back I asked him, "Why you held it down for dudes when dudes snitched on you?"

He simply replied, "Tee, I wasn't brought up like that, I'll just do my time."

There was nothing else to be said. Only respect to be given. I am in no way glorifying or condoning his alleged past behavior. I'm just clearly saying that if you're gonna talk about it, be about it. If you're gonna partake in certain illegal activities then be a man and stand up when those boys come for you. Everybody wants to be a part of something, but when it's time to pay for it, they start shifting the blame to someone else. Half these niggas need to piss sitting down. SMH!!!

Don't get me wrong. You don't have to indulge in gangsta life to prove that you're a man either. Be a productive citizen in society by educating yourself, working an honest job, or starting a business and taking care of your family and your community. That's more gangsta to me than anything. And let me say this, there are a lot of forty and fifty year old teenagers running these streets with their pants sagging. Ya'll clowns driving BMW's and Benz', but don't have your own apartments, don't have credit, but want to be respected as grown men. GTFOH!!!! Ya'll look crazy. Straight up. Please don't think nobody's talking about you behind your back. I'm saying it loud and clear.

At the same time, I realized that a lot of my black men can't read, which is one of the main reasons why ya'll turn to the streets in the first place. But please don't let that continue to be a reason not to do better. Man up, admit what you don't know and just ask for help. It's okay to acknowledge you need help and ask for it. That's gangsta. What's not ok is you bringing children into this world and can't even help them with simple shit like their homework. That's not ok. You must do better for yourselves and your children. I'll respect that street image over any drug deal, murder or any amount of money you have in your stash.

Lou Sims: Gangsta Lou

I would never condone what they say Lou did. At the same time, I don't know what is or isn't true about everything that has been said. Like I mentioned before everybody has a hustle. Allegedly, Lou's hustle was putting fear into people, and it worked. Actually, some people were just scared for no damn reason.

People make decisions in their lives that they'll have to live with forever. Lou was no different. Does he have regrets? Sure he does. Is he living with them? Sure he is. He doesn't want anyone trying to be or act like him. He never wanted to be away from his family and children, but loyalty meant everything to him and that may have been his downfall.

He doesn't want anyone glorifying what the media said he allegedly did. Whatever Lou did, he stood alone. Can ya'll? Are ya'll really ready to do the time? Are ya'll ready for the consequences? In 1995 Lou got thirty years plus the electric chair. If you can deal with that shit, then maybe ya'll are gangsta.

According to the indictment, he was responsible for the deaths of a lot of people. And by responsible, the authorities believed that if he didn't do it himself, others killed under his direction. When the FEDS snatched Lou up it was all over the papers and in the news. Reportedly, the murder rate in Harlem went down 56% after he got arrested. Let that marinate for a minute and then do the math. 56%? I say it's bullshit. That's a hell of a reputation to carry around. I'm sure Mary Jo White, the United States Attorney at the time, exaggerated a bit. This man was being blamed for more than half the murders that occurred in the borough. That's insane. That's a street image I wouldn't want. As you can see there is a price to pay when your name is ringing bells in the street like that.

One of the headlines read, "Drug Gang Dies and Harlem Comes Alive."

WHOA!!!! That's crazy. Also on his indictment was an attempt on my life, not by him, but we'll talk about that later.

Is Lou the monster the media and the police portrayed him to be, or is he just misunderstood? Was he a product of his environment? Maybe he was a scapegoat for the crimes of others. Maybe he was just loyal to those who later turned their backs on him. Maybe he's the true meaning of what a real comrade is. There are only a few people who really know this individual and what he stood for. I knew him as someone different. I knew the person who loved life. He loved to have fun and tell corny ass jokes. I had the pleasure of knowing, loving and experiencing the cool person he really is. He's my ex-boyfriend and best friend. He's also a loving father, brother, uncle and grandfather.

The media reported him as Lou Griffin, aka Lou Sims, aka Homicide Lou, aka Supreme; and called his alleged crew the Lynch Mob. But to me, he's just Boola, a nickname I gave him back in 1989.

Lou and I

I've known Lou since I was around five, six, or maybe seven years old. He and my family go way back. He ran the streets with my cousin Ronnie Ball, my Aunt Myrtle's son, when they were teenagers. There's no telling what their activities entailed back then, but I imagine they did some wild shit. Anyway, a lot of years passed where I didn't see him. Of course he spent some of those years in jail. And then I bumped into him one day in '89. I was all grown up then. I didn't remember much about him, but the one thing I did remember was that he wasn't to be fucked with. How I remembered something like that from a child is crazy, but that much I did remember.

Summer was approaching and I was walking up 8th Avenue on my way from the cleaners when I saw a red car slowing down. It was a Mazda MX-6.

"What's up Tonia?" Lou yelled out the car window.

His fine ass was in the car with his man from uptown, I heard that Lou hung out with him. I had also heard that Lou had gotten out of prison a few years earlier, but I hadn't seen him yet. I remember thinking that day, "Is that that nigga Lou?" Yup, that was his fine ass.

"What's up?" I answered back.

So there he was looking at me, and I was looking at him. We just smiled at each other for a moment. Like I said, it had been years since we saw each other and I was a kid back then. I was surprised he even remembered me, but I figured homie in the car must've spotted me and told him who I was. I thought I was cute that day and I was sure acting like it too. He smiled, I smiled and then he drove off.

"Yeah I'll get him," I said to myself as I watched the car pull away. I later found out he was thinking the same thing.

Before I go on, anybody that really knows Lou knows he be clownin'. He and I had a conversation while I was writing this, and he remembered what I had on that day and everything. I didn't even recall all that, but I knew I was dressed. He said I had on a two-piece, blue silk suit, which was probably true because I loved silk, and thong sandals. Then he went on to say that my toes looked like burnt French Fries. LIES!!! My toes don't look like that ya'll just in case he tries to tell somebody this story. LMAO.

Now, back to how I swept that MF off his feet. LOL. I knew I would see Lou again, and I knew I would get him, but I didn't know that his alleged hidden occupation would one day be exposed. That day, I figured he was on his way to see his man Tee Money on 127th Street. The streets talked and I had heard him and Tee were cool too, but Tee wasn't even around because he was in Florida with my cousin Shelli at that time, I believe.

Tee and his crew had 127th & 8th Ave on lock. There was another wild dude that used to be down there too. His name was Blackie. He was a real dark Dominican that kept some paper. He always had nice cars. One of them was a yellow Lamborghini. I was fascinated by that car. Allegedly, Blackie was one of the major connects.

Anyway, Lou and I started talking that summer. He started coming around more often, visiting me and we ended up spending a lot of time together. He actually had a girl when we first got together. He told me he lived with her somewhere Upstate, but that didn't really matter to me or him, obviously. She was there, I was here, and he was with me. Back then I didn't care about shit like that. I was young and I wanted what I wanted. His situation didn't seem to matter to him, so why should I have cared?

You see, pussy was and will always be a powerful thing and not all pussy is the same, from what I hear. It's like a bag of heroin. Hit them with that eight and a motherfucker is guaranteed to nod off. Lou and I had a very intense sexual relationship. When it comes to good pussy, it'll make some men do some crazy shit. It can make a man do the unexpected like leave his family, give you all his money, and even kill for you. Oh yeah, kill your ass too. LOL. I recognized the power of the "P" at an early age, perfected my craft, and ran with it. HEY!!! We just talking ya'll. Right? So I have to put it out there.

Anyway, one day while me and Lou were in bed, Dog called from prison. I felt guilty talking to him while I had another guy lying right next to me butt ass naked, but Lou lay there quietly, respecting our fifteen minute conversation, which was how long we got before the phone automatically cut off. I had four more years until Dog came home, so I had to do me. I was young and waiting five years for a dude to get out of prison, seemed like a lifetime at 19 years old.

If dudes thought that their chicks weren't cheating on them while they were away, they were lying to themselves, especially if they were doing FED time. Only the State had conjugal visits, so you figure it out. There are some good women out there, but if that chick was use to a certain kind of lifestyle and the guy didn't leave any money behind, then they got cheated on. POINT BLANK!!! Especially back in the day when that street money was plentiful.

Lou and his crew were gettin' money. When we first got together, he thought I was working for Stan and that we were getting major money. The streets talk too much. I guess the way I dressed and carried myself told a bigger story than reality, but it wasn't that serious. Some people knew that I hustled, but I got a lot of my money from dudes and this sweet Jamaican named Phil. Phil use to have bags of money. He'd just open one of those bags and tell me to take what I wanted. YO!!!! And I did. He offered to buy me a BMW, but for some strange reason I was reluctant. YES! ME!! RELUCTANT!!! I know it's hard to believe. He was on me so hard that I thought a car would be like a ring of marriage or some shit. Ya'll know how some Jamaicans can be real possessive and I didn't want to feel obligated to him. I was 18 at that time. I liked him, but I liked his money more. LOL.

My mother was also responsible for a lot that I had. But when all else failed there was Stan who gave me everything I asked for. I hustled here and there and sold this and that from time to time and I guess Lou took that for more than it was and thought he was going to get access to Stan's connect through me or something, so I heard. But I was a little smarter than that. I was very protective of Stan. It wouldn't have been easy getting anything out of me. When Lou realized that it wasn't what he thought, he let it go. Although, initially it may not have been in his plans to really get involved with me, he did. One day he said, "I thought ya'll had some money, ya'll ain't have shit." LMAO. Funny MF.

Lou and I were cool. He was my baby. We had a lot of fun together. My aunt would go out drinking and come to my mom's house and fall out and me and Lou would sneak her keys and go to her house and do what young people do. We had fun at my house too, playing and taking pictures. Some people don't know that side of him.

We argued from time to time about me wanting things. I was a brat so when I asked for something I expected it right then and there. One thing I can say is that when I screamed, he listened. So when I needed something and he didn't have the money, I still got it. I guess it was nice to have access to other people's money, whether they liked it or not, sometimes whether they knew it or not. It was either give it up or give it up. Doesn't really sound like much of a choice does it? Nah, I'm just playing…. Am I? Hmmmmm.

It seemed like everybody respected him and that was exciting, but I often wondered whether it was respect or something else.

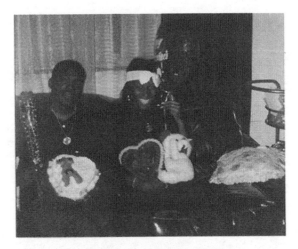

Me and Lou Valentines Day

Lou and Lil Sis acting silly

Lou and I in the Poconos
He's trying to look mean. Lol

WTF

Although I try to protect my people no matter what because of loyalty and respect I know they weren't saints. I know they indulged in activities that they shouldn't have. The truth is I often found myself wondering, "Why was Lou's name always associated with something bad?" He was my man and I wasn't going anywhere. Unfortunately, that meant the consequences of his decisions sometimes fell on me. I remember this one afternoon Lou called me and told me to come downstairs so we could go out to eat.

"Give me a minute. I have to take a shower," I told him.

"I'll be waiting in front of the building," he said.

I hopped in the shower and was getting dressed when a guy I knew from the block knocked on my door.

"Lou's downstairs arguing with some dude," he said.

Before I could finish getting dressed, I heard gunshots. I ran to my back window and it was like something out of the movies. People were screaming, running, ducking and hiding. Witnesses later said there were two men shooting at each other from a half a block away from each other. All that on 8th Ave. GOD must've been on both their sides because neither of them got hit. I couldn't believe that shit happened in broad daylight. Then again, I could believe it. Anyway, I finished getting dressed and hurried out the house.

I was shocked, scared and in disbelief all at the same time when I rushed outside to see what was going on. I wanted to make sure Lou wasn't laying outside in a pool of blood. I stepped out the building and was greeted by so many stares you would've thought I had a gun in my hand. At first I was like, "Why the hell ya'll looking at me like that?" But then I remembered that I was the girl that was going out with the crazy nigga that just shot up the block.

By the time I got downstairs, Lou had already jumped in his car and went uptown, which was the smart thing to do because I lived right around the corner from the precinct. I went back upstairs and paged him after being raped by all those stares. He called me back to say that he was okay, but the dinner date was off. I guess all that excitement made him lose his appetite. I didn't want to walk back out the building anyway. After that incident a lot of people from my block kept their distance from me. Even the ones I grew up with. They didn't want any parts of what happened. I could dig it though. You should be cautious with things that could be hazardous to your health and talking to me or messing with me could've been just that.

I later found out that the incident was over a dice game that went bad. That's crazy, right ya'll? But then again, a lot of dudes from hoods all over have been killed over a dice game gone wrong. A dice game can be detrimental to a Black man's health. Instead of playing the game, guys concentrate on egos, money and talking shit; and the next thing you know, the guns are drawn. And there's no coming back from that. The guy that argued with Lou obviously had no idea who he was dealing with. Maybe he didn't even care.

In a lot of ways, a dice game in the streets is a game of life and death. Dice games draw out all kinds of characters: from dudes that just join the game to front, to dudes that join the game with intentions to straight jack the game and rob everybody. It's unfortunate that a simple game consisting of two little square pieces of plastic can cause so much loss of life. Think about it Black men. Get your shit together. It's supposed to be a fun game.

Needless to say, I was worried for Lou after that. I didn't know what to do or what to think. I didn't want anyone to come back to try to kill him. I feared for his life quite often. He didn't seem to worry much about anything, but I think I was worried enough for the both of us. He showed absolutely no fear. I knew that if I was going to stay with that man, I had to prepare for a bumpy ride, but did I want that?

Who? I Don't Know That MF

One day me and my girls were driving uptown to the Polo Grounds to take Lou's grandmother something to eat from Sylvia's. Sylvia's was and still is a famous soul food restaurant in Harlem. Lou's grandmother Jo was my girl. She loved him so much. He was the baby out of 10 brothers and sisters, and she spoiled him. She use to call him Mr. Louis. She was too cute. Sometimes he and I stayed with her to keep her company. Anyway when we were passing 154th and 8th Ave we heard gunshots. I knew from the number of shots somebody got hit. In the hood you can estimate whether somebody just got hit or just got killed by the number of shots you heard.

So, I parked, dropped the food off to Jo and me and my girls walked around the corner to see what happened and learned that this guy named John John from the Bronx got killed. I had heard about him in the streets. He was from Edenwald Projects, but he hung out on Amsterdam Avenue sometimes. I had no idea what he was doing on 8th Avenue that night and really didn't care, but I had heard a lot about him. I heard that he had a lot of dudes scared on the streets, and there had been several unsuccessful attempts on his life. Some people thought he couldn't get killed. They use to say he had nine lives. I guess that nine ran out. His body was lying between 8th Ave and Bradhurst and a crowd had already gathered around the scene.

"They finally got him," I couldn't help thinking.

As the crowd grew, me and my girls started back to the rental car I had, ready to go back downtown. Before I could get to the car, two detectives walked straight up to me.

One of them pointed to John John's body. "Miss do you know that Man?"

"No," I said and started walking off.

They were like, "Miss someone pointed you out and said he got out of this car with you".

"No the fuck he didn't. I don't even know him."

"Miss you need to come with us," they insisted.

"This is some bullshit," I complained. "Listen officers, I just came from my grandmother's, came to be nosey and now I'm going home."

"You can come with us, or we can arrest you," they threatened.

I held my wrist out. "Then break out the fuckin' cuffs."

Those MF's were putting me in a dangerous situation. The killers could've still been out there and what would they have thought if I just willingly got into that police car? It was four of us, but they only took two of us. They took me and my friend to the 32nd precinct and put us in different rooms. They made us write statements about everything we did for the previous two hours. I had no problem with that. I wrote down everything we did. I left nothing out. It was a full legal size page. My friend's statement was half that. I don't know why, but she left a lot of shit out. I remember thinking, WTF! After looking at the disparity between our stories, they went crazy on me. I kind of knew something was up then, but I kept my cool.

"Can I call my lil sister? She was with me earlier," I told them.

They called her up to verify who she was, picked her up from the house, and brought her to the precinct and questioned her about what we did earlier that night. She was only fourteen years old at the time. Her statement matched mine, so they had to let us go. But before they did they sat me at a table and dropped a stack of photos in front of me. They were old black and white mug shots of dudes I didn't know.

"Who are they?" I asked.

"You know."

I looked closely and saw that one of the photos was of Lou. He looked so young I almost didn't recognize him. I kept a straight face, laughing my ass off inside. I knew they were on some bullshit when they pressed me about him.

"You know him don't you?" one of the detectives asked

pointing at the photo.

"Ya'll seem to know everything. Ya'll tell me who it is."

They looked at each other and burst out laughing. I didn't get the joke. I was really confused. I didn't see a damn thing funny except for that old ass photo of Lou. I walked out of there freely, but I knew something just wasn't right. They were probably trying to get me to talk about his street activities. It's funny because I didn't know anything anyway, but even if I did I still wouldn't have said anything. They had to have been following me from the beginning. They never picked me up for John John. I think it was a coincidence that John John got killed while they were on my ass, which gave their crooked asses the opportunity to take me in. Slick MF's!!!!

I immediately paged Lou when I got home. He was mad. Not because they asked about him, but because they picked me up and held me for some bullshit. I was wondering what it was that they wanted with him. I was clueless. Whether they believed me or not, I really didn't know anything. Lou never talked to me about his business. As a matter of fact, he never discussed any of his business on the streets with me period. That's how it should be, although there are some exceptions. If a dude got a chick that doesn't understand the streets, the less she knows the better. On the other hand, it's only right to have a chick that knows the streets and can act fast in a crisis. She has to know how to act fast under pressure. When shit gets thick you gotta know how to stand your ground and shut the fuck up. The police don't know nothing if you don't say nothing; most of the time. They speculate a lot.

I was always that chick that dudes could talk to. Although I'm not in that life I still get calls from dudes living the life looking for nothing more than a listening ear. They know I can still relate and give them the advice they need. Hopefully some of them will finally realize the game is over.

For the most part I knew things were going down, but at that time Lou told me nothing. I didn't know why those cops wanted to mess with Lou. I didn't care what he was into. I was just in to him. Things were happening. Bodies were dropping here and there and the only name I began to hear was my boyfriends' name. Lou Sims.

R.I.P Grandma Jo

Back To Life: 1989

It was the year Soul II Soul came out with "Back to Life" and "Keep on Moving." Now you know when that beat dropped on "Back to Life," that was it. That was like the theme song that summer. Every car that drove up and down the Ave was pumping that song. And yes, that summer was off the hook.

Although Stan was married, he had started messing with a girl named Tammy. She and I knew of each other because we lived in the same area, but we eventually became real close, which put me in a bad situation with Stan's wife. Stan was always putting me in bad situations with his shenanigans. And those shenanigans always involved him messing with other chicks. I loved my aunt, but I'm sure my loyalty to Stan made it hard for her to trust or probably even like me at times. MF always had me in the middle of his shit.

That summer my girls and I were driving down to Virginia Beach for Labor Day. The whole Harlem was going and I invited Tammy to go with us. Stan wasn't too happy about that. He didn't want her to go. Lou wasn't mad that I was going, but then that's probably because he was up to his own shenanigans. So on the night we were leaving; Tammy, Lou, Stan, and I went to eat at the Chinese restaurant on 121st and 8th Avenue. Do ya'll remember that spot? The food was good and they were the first spot that had the extra-large ice teas. Well anyway, this nigga Stan acted a fool up in there. He threw one of those big ass ice teas all over Tammy's clothes. I didn't know what the hell was wrong with him, but if he thought some ice tea and wet clothes were stopping the show he had another thing coming. That shit was hilarious though. He didn't want his boo to leave. Tammy had him wide open, but she wasn't about to miss that trip. We went anyway and had a ball.

Whoever went down there that year has to remember how

off the hook it was. It got so crazy down there that they called in the National Guard and gave us a curfew. I've never seen anything like it. The police were chasing dudes and beating their asses. At that time Shelli was driving a gold Acura Legend that belonged to her new boyfriend Jamaican Tony from Edgecombe. Anyway, Shelli was driving down some dead end street in VA because the streets were crowded with people, the police, and the National Guard. Some dude came out of nowhere and jumped in her back seat. Just as fast as he jumped in she took the keys and jumped out and started screaming at this fool to get out. He did and kept on running.

Everybody was mad about the curfew and trashed the hotels in protest. They threw TVs off of balconies and hurled fire extinguishers at the police. It was crazy as hell, but we still had fun. Unfortunately, no matter how much I try to describe certain people, places, and events; I'll never be able to give you the full experience of being there. And to really understand how crazy it was in Virginia Beach that year, you had to have been there. It was like a war zone. But no matter the circumstances, we had a ball. No matter what we did or where we went, we represented.

Gots To Be More Careful

Virginia was definitely an experience, but I missed my baby. Unfortunately, Lou wasn't the only thing waiting for me when I got home. It was about two weeks after my trip, summer was coming to an end, and there was nothing but drama.

"What the hell happened to Melvin?" I thought to myself when I got the call that they found Lou's friend dead uptown. I can't remember who called me. I always got a call when someone got killed in the streets. My mothers' number was hot. Everybody knew that Goddamn number. A lot of the times Shelli and I would be standing there when shit went down. Don't even ask me why? Why the HELL they called me? I don't know. Although I was always lady like, I think me being around Stan and the fellas made me like one of the guys. In some ways he ruined me, but that's another story.

Anyway, I knew Lou was going to be mad as hell, but he handled it better than I expected. I'll never forget how he responded when I inquired about the Melvin situation.

"Don't forget we're going Upstate to see Blue tomorrow," was his simple reply.

I guess that was his way of telling me to mind my business. Maybe he dealt with sorrow in his own way, I thought. Everybody deals with a loss differently and maybe he thought he had to play tough all the time. Or was it something else? Gots to be more careful! The next day Lou and I drove Upstate. It was a ride we made often. We would visit his nephew Blue, his man Bogart and this other dude in prison. For many of those trips, I transported weed compressed and stuffed in balloons. When we got on the visit floor, I got whoever we were visiting a soda, passed them the balloons of weed when the coast was clear, and then watched them put it in their mouth and swallow it down with a soda. After the visit, they went back to their cell and shitted the balloon out. Ewww. I'm not digging through any shit to find anything unless it's a big diamond or a key to a safe full of money.

Lou was good and loyal to his people in prison. He had been in their position before and knew how hard it could be in there without help from the outside. The weed allowed them to make enough money on the inside to sustain for a while. He tried his best to make sure that they were okay. So we took that trip at least once a month. The other dude we visited was one of Lou's good friends that ended up snitching on him a few years later allegedly when the Lynch Mob was shut down. SMH!!! I won't mention his name. When he got out, he chose not to come back to N.Y. Damn!!! He lost his dignity, and can't even see his family and kids. Was it worth it? Gots to be more careful with who you call friends out here.

Thinking back, I really risked my own freedom taking drugs up there like that. I wasn't forced to do it, but I guess I loved Lou that much that I would have done anything that he asked me to. Or did I just like breaking laws? Maybe I just didn't realize what I was doing and how much trouble I could have gotten into. I don't recommend that any woman risk their freedom doing that for anyone. It's wrong no matter how you look at it. No man is worth doing this for. **NO MAN**

Me, Lou, Blue Bogart

What Goes Around Comes Around

Unfortunately Jacob's day finally came in 1990. He was killed while he was on a pay phone on 8th Avenue. Yes, the same Jacob that allegedly set Al up back in 1986. From what I heard, someone decided to avenge Al's death. That someone was allegedly Al's best friend. I'll just call him Cutie, and that he was.

I'll never forget the night of Jacob's wake. Me, Lou, Stan, and a few other dudes were standing in front on my building on 8th Avenue when all hell broke loose. Ya'll have to picture this. There was scaffolding around my building because they were doing some work on the roof. Stan stood under the scaffolding talking to some guys from the block. My friend Michelle and her man were standing on 134th Street with the car door open with music playing. Lou and I stood between 133rd & 134th, on the curve talking next to the fire hydrant.

We were all just hanging out. I was facing the street and Lou was facing me. We were just standing there talking when all of a sudden a strange look came over Lou's face. He was looking towards 134th street. He slowly stepped off the curve and into the street and I turned to see what caught his attention. Everything happened so fast, but yet in slow motion. I saw three or four guys with hoodies and guns.

"There that motherfucker go," one of them yelled out.

And then there was a hail of gunfire and chaos. Lou pushed me and ran off thinking the gunmen were after him, but they ran straight trying to assassinate Stan. The two dudes with Stan took off running, and one got shot in the ass. All I could do is yell, scream, and wonder what the fuck was going on. I was scared and confused at the same time. Why were they after Stan?

I was hysterical, wondering if Stan was lying somewhere

dead. He ran up to St. Nicholas Park and vanished. I jumped in my friend's car and he drove me and my friend over to Amsterdam Ave to see if Stan ran over there, but there was no sign of him. I came back to the park and yelled his name out, but got no answer. I went back to my building and went upstairs to page him. When I got there, I found Stan and Lou in the apartment. Lou was freaking out, mad as hell and ready to hurt something.

Stan sat there with a blank and confused look on his face. I'm sure he couldn't believe what just happened. We were all wondering the same thing. "Who the hell was that?" Did it have something to do with Jacob? Jacob wasn't even in the ground yet and somebody was avenging his death. But why come after Stan.

Lou was putting on his bullet proof vest and gearing up for war. What war? I didn't know. Stan was undecided about what to do next, but it was clear to Lou that someone had to pay for what just happened, but who? If Jacob was dead, who were the shooters? I wondered if it even had anything to do with Jacob?

One night Tee Money was sitting in his car on 127th Street when someone showed up out of nowhere blasting their gun. The gunman hit Tee Money and an innocent passenger that was in the car. Both of them died. Was this the same gunman that chased Stan down I wondered? Shit was getting crazy.

It came out that the alleged shooter that night was Jacob's little brother. Jacob meant the world to him and I respect the way he went out for his big brother. Lil Bro was on a warpath avenging his brother's death. The wrath of Lil Bro continued as he went through Harlem like a mad man with a team of little dudes ridin' with him. Jacob died and Lil Bro was going to make sure that everyone he thought was involved would die too. He gave a new meaning to "Am I my brother's keeper?" Was Lil Bro wrong about this? I really don't know. But he wasn't done yet.

The saga continued one day in front of Mart 125, Cutie met his fate in broad daylight. He stood on the street, not expecting to see Lil Bro. What was about to happen would have Harlem talking for weeks. With the quickness, Lil Bro drew his gun and got the drop on Cutie. I heard he shot Cutie in both legs, bringing him to his knees. With his hand on his gun a second too late, Cutie looked up at Lil Bro in fear and disappointment that he got caught out there. Lil

Bro fired one more shot to Cutie's head and chest, and Cutie was dead. Lil Bro had avenged his brothers' death.

Lil Bro's killing spree soon came to an end, along with his own life. There were all kinds of rumors about how he was killed. One story said a man wearing a dress and pushing a baby stroller walked up and killed him. I'm not even going to tell ya'll who they say had that dress on. SMH!!!!

So, what was it all over? Was Jacob's death over some pussy? Was it payback for something he did to someone? It seems like more than a few people had a reason to dislike Jacob. Whatever it was; was it all worth it? Although Lil Bro lost his life, I'm sure for him, that killing spree was well worth making sure Jacob rested in peace knowing that his little brother was there for him to avenge his death.

I'm just glad that I didn't get caught up in the line of fire. If Lou wasn't out there that night, most likely I would've been standing right next to Stan.

Too Much To Handle

Lou took loyalty to heart, and he was a good and loyal friend to Fat Boy from uptown. I had known Fat Boy for a while and loved him with all my heart. We were like family. He was real cool and funny as hell. I would do anything for him and he would do the same for me. He and Lou were real tight. Lou was like his *handyman*, allegedly. Anybody who disrespected Fat Boy or owed him money had to answer to Lou. After Melvin passed away, Lou started spending a lot more time with Fat Boy. They had a nice clique uptown. According to the media, this clique called themselves the Lynch Mob. They had their block on Lenox Avenue on lock, but they had a knucklehead or two in their crew that ran around doing dumb shit with no repercussions because people knew who they were down with. That dumb shit was most likely what brought the so called Lynch Mob down.

Lou continued to get a bad rap on the streets. They blamed him for every dude that ended up dead. I remember when Rich Porter was killed. I got a threatening phone call from some unknown person.

"Yeah bitch, we know Lou did it and they're gonna find your ass in the river," the caller said.

I couldn't believe it. ME!!!! I remember wondering, "If they think Lou did it, what the fuck does that have to do with me?"

I'll never forget that phone call. Lou wasn't the person they were trying to make him out to be, or so I thought. When people thought of him they thought of a person that probably never smiled, never laughed, never told corny jokes, and didn't like to have fun, which was far from the truth. You had to be close enough to him to know it, but he was a good guy. My family and friends enjoyed being around him too. Maine admired him and wanted to be just like him.

Lou had this persona of being a very dangerous and unapproachable person, but he really wasn't. Love and honor for his fellow comrades was what later became his downfall. Yes he was a no nonsense type of guy, but he had a good heart. He wasn't a serial killer or anything like that, so why the hell was my life being threatened and why were people blaming every murder on him?

I knew Lou didn't kill Rich, but being from the streets, I knew that accusation had to be addressed and without violence. I waited for him to come in that night and told him what happened. I needed him to go to Rich's block to talk to Rich's people to straighten that shit out. I had more life to live and I wasn't getting killed for no one else's bullshit. Plus there was already an ongoing FBI investigation into the kidnapping of Rich's little brother a few weeks earlier. I knew this had to be dealt with IMMEDIATELY!

Lou was furious. He immediately went back outside, but before he left I asked him to put on a bulletproof vest. You never know what could happen. I didn't want him going out unprepared. There was always one cocky motherfucker in the group that felt he had something to prove.

He returned quickly and said that everything was cool. He never said whether he had spoken to anyone or not. But when he said everything was okay, I took his word for it. That's when I realized that maybe someone was playing around. I still took the call serious because it meant someone close to us was wishing us harm. I also realized that people were just hating on him by always putting his name in shit. Who the hell could have called me with those threats? Rich's people didn't have my number, but then again people had been known to pay for my phone number. SMH!!! It had to be someone close. It's always someone close. It was probably someone in Lou's own crew. There's always someone hating from the sidelines. But who?

I knew I had to start protecting myself. I had a gun that Unique had given me. I hadn't so much as looked at it since we broke up, but I felt it was time to start carrying it. It was a very shiny, silver, .380 with a pearl handle. It was brand new. It was the cutest thing I had ever seen. I never really carried it out, but I was glad to know it was there in case I needed it. Like I said before I wasn't ready to die for no one else's bullshit.

I started taking heed and paying more attention to the things I was hearing on the streets about Lou. They were saying some crazy and serious shit. On one hand it got me to thinking about what it meant if some of the shit was true, but on the other hand it was exciting to me. I wasn't happy that people were getting killed, but being with someone that everyone feared gave me a kind of rush. I was young and didn't realize the ramifications of what could happen to me because of simply being in a relationship with someone people thought was a stone-cold killer.

I remember this boyfriend I had a few years before getting with Lou. Me and my girls were out one night when we bumped into my then boyfriend and his man. I took one look at them and instantly knew that something was up. I mean, it was summer and these dudes had on black hoodies.

"What's up?" I nosily asked my boyfriend.

"Go home," he flatly answered.

Me being me, I stayed and told the girls that something was about to go down. And it did. It went down a few minutes later. My boyfriend and his man threw the hoods over their heads, ran across the street to a small crowd of guys, and laid this one dude out.

The point is that's the kind of men I found myself with. Was it me? Why did I seem to attract bad guys? Why couldn't I get a nice guy that liked to play ball and just kick it? Why was I excited by all the craziness? Is that what I wanted my life to be? Surely it wasn't what my parents wanted for me, but time and time again, that's where I found myself. This type of lifestyle was becoming too much too handle.

Should I Leave Him?

Another thing about being with a hustler or gangster back then was that there were always other women. Sometimes men had to lay their heads from place to place. Instead of getting their own apartment, they just paid a chick to stay at her apartment. It was a survival tactic, I guess. They always had to be a step ahead of the bad guys. Sometimes they were the bad guys. At the same time, it was easy to get an apartment back in the day because you could pay under the table. So some dudes did have their own spots. Although it often started with dudes paying chicks to stay in their apartments to bottle up drugs or lay their heads, those arrangements sometimes grew into relationships. Those different apartments and relationships with different women often resulted in dudes having children with different women. For the most part we had to just charge it to the game. That's just how things were.

I remember I got a call one day from a chick that lived uptown where Lou hung out. She told me that Lou was messing with a girl from up there. I had already suspected that his black ass was cheating on me, but I didn't know with whom. He came home right after I got off the phone with the chick. I went off and threatened to leave him. It was then that I realized that he was off the hook. I told him I knew everything and raised my hand to slap him. That was my first mistake. We began to fight. I yelled and screamed through the house. It was so loud that my neighbors knocked on the door. He grabbed me and slammed me to the floor. I was scared as hell, but I managed to get back on my feet. It was like he blacked out and didn't realize what he was doing or who I was. We struggled and I tried to take the gun he had in his waistband, but he was quicker than me. I was scared because he didn't look like himself. He laid the gun down, grabbed my arm with a wicked smile on his face, twisted my arm until I fell to the floor again, and then kicked me in my chest. I couldn't believe that MF.

"He's the one that got caught cheating, not me," I thought.

He let me go and opened the door to find a butch chick that lived across the hall holding a machete. The sight of her didn't faze him one bit. Another one of my neighbors was in the hall too, screaming and cursing his ass out. He paid her no mind. He bopped to the elevator like no one could do him any harm.

Later on that night, my cousin Shelli and her man took me to the hospital. I was okay, but I just needed to be sure. The next day I found out that Lou went uptown and slapped the girl that told me, but that wasn't it. He also beat up her brother and was about to give their moms the business too. That was when I finally admitted that he was out of control, and I needed to get away. But how? And Why? I loved him. I knew he didn't mean to hurt me. I guess the thought of me ending our relationship made him crazy. Or maybe it was just that his ass got busted. MF's always try to flip the script when they get busted. I should've heard his side of the story before threatening to end our relationship. That's how I rationalized it at the time, but deep down inside I knew it was all true.

I still stayed with him, but I never forgot the look on his face that night. It was like he didn't know who I was. I decided to give him another chance, but you better believe I made him sweat a bit first. He and I had already made plans to go to the Poconos, and I had been excited about going, but I started to play like I didn't want to go, knowing damn well I did. I remember he went complaining to my mother. I thought that was so cute. He begged me to go and I gave in.

I was getting tired of the news about other girls though. Then there was the baby he and his girl Upstate was having. Lou was a ladies' man. He loved women and they loved him, but that didn't mean I had to deal with the bullshit. I just kept asking myself, "Should I leave him?"

We ended up taking that ride to the Poconos and it was great. We really enjoyed it. We both needed that quiet time together, but was it enough for him to stop his bullshit? Black ass MF. LOL

A Woman's Worth

Ladies do you know your worth? Do you know that your life is not defined by the kind of man you're with? Do you know that your life is not defined by the kind of job that you do? Your character tells everything about you. Are you genuine? Are you loyal? Are you honest? Or are you one of those trifling chicks with no morals? You know the type that'll sleep with your friend's man. Are you the type that'll smile all up in your girl's face, but be hating on her from the sidelines because she has more than you have or she has the kind of man you want? Girl stop. Know your worth.

Never let a man define who you are. Never let a man tarnish your character. These days, you don't need a man for anything. Excuse me, but BITCHES are running shit these days. I'm not bashing men at all, but they've been allowed to disrespect women for far too long. No one has held them accountable for their behavior. You have to start holding them accountable by not accepting the names they call you. Make them check the bullshit at the door. Why would you let your man come home after you know he's been out with the next chick? Because he's cute? Because he has a few dollars? Yeah, but a lot of times he's also dumb as a rock. Girls, get your life and make him constantly qualify to be in it. And when he doesn't meet your qualifications, send him on his way. But if you're one of those trifling chicks, you're not really in a position to set qualifications and standards and your dude will probably treat you how your hand calls for.

If you're not educated and your options are limited then that ain't nobody's fault but yours. Let me guess, you have no choice but to accept what a man does to you, right? Hell nah. Get it together. It's never too late. I may have done the streets, but I got two degrees and I ain't never been no man's fool. Every once and a while we all fall short and do dumb shit. The key is getting back up, knowing what you're worth and keeping it pushing.

Although I had relationships with different dudes, I never let any one of them define who I was. My exes will tell you, "Tee would stick and move on your ass quick." There was never enough money that would make me accept disrespect from a dude. NO AMOUNT!!! That's for those birds. Know your worth. Even though I described what I went through with Lou, he was one of the people that told me and continues to tell me to never let any man disrespect me.

I remember I met this one chick back in 1999 when I lived in Glenwood Gardens in Yonkers. She was a heavy girl with a beautiful face and had struggled with her weight since she was a kid. She had female cousins that dealt with drug dealers and had been involved with fast money. She told me she wished she could experience the fast life and being with a drug dealer. I explained to her that there was also a dark side to that life. Things aren't always what they seem. I mean, it was lovely not having to always worry about money or bills, driving around with my girls, having a good time on vacations, and having the man that every other girl wanted. But I had to put her up on the not so good times. It wasn't all sweet. What about the chick that had to endure the cheater because she had nowhere to go or not enough skill to do it on her own? What about the chick that endured beatings and stayed because she misconstrued the abuse for love? I had to school this girl on the reality that some people don't make it out the game, including women. I don't think she had given that any thought at all. I haven't seen her in a while, but I hope she's doing well.

Women can be stupid sometimes too. We all know when something is going on with our man. Men aren't that smooth or smart when they're cheating. There is nothing like a woman's intuition. Some of us just choose to play dumb and accept our men cheating and lying to us. I've never been that chick. Chicks like that need to get their lives together. Then again, if you're a chick that has absolutely nothing going for yourself it's understandable why you stay. You have no options. Options are a beautiful thing.

So, go to school my ladies. Learn a skill and educate yourselves. This way when a dude gets stupid you can give him your ass to kiss instead of letting him play you, play on you and end up giving you AIDS or some shit like that. Step your game up ladies. Start showing these silly ass men that it's not all about them or their money; it can be about you too. We can get our own money and trick on ourselves.

My point to her and my point to all you ladies out there is that you need to remember that you're the most precious thing that you can give to a man. You have to make sure he knows it, believes it and respects it.

Fritz: The Consignment King

The summer of 1990 had just begun and I started going downtown to 112th Street with Tammy to see her "play" uncle. Her intentions were to go down there so we could get money to hang, but we ended up hanging out down there a lot. Her uncle was cool. He seemed like a regular dude. He wore t-shirts, acid wash jeans and didn't wear jewelry, but little did I know, he was that NIGGA!

His name was **FRITZ**.

At the time I had no idea who he was. It turned out that, allegedly, he was the biggest cocaine supplier in Harlem. This allegedly shit is getting hilarious, but it has to be done. LOL. Fritz was a certified "hood millionaire." He was known as the richest man in Harlem. He was a Kingpin. He was the Consignment King. Ya'll remember I told ya'll about how consignment works right? Everybody had the opportunity to get money because of Fritz. He was known to be very generous and he was. He believed that anyone and everyone who wanted to hustle should be given a chance to do so. Directly or indirectly, he was the reason bosses were made in Harlem. He was the source behind many crews in Harlem getting money back in the eighties and early nineties. If you purchased drugs from someone other than him, it was a huge chance it still came from him.

In the beginning Tammy and I hung out in front of his apartment building when we went down there, but I remember clearly the first time she took me up to the apartment. I saw him and another guy at a table counting money and neatly packing it in a bag. I thought to myself, "I love Stan, but Fritz could be my uncle too."

If you saw him you wouldn't think he was the King of anything, but he was. I can say he was the KING of HARLEM. Who wants to dispute that? He made me a true believer in the saying; "you must never judge a book by its cover." That cover definitely didn't tell the story of a man who had an asshole full of money. Still, even though he was filthy rich, he wasn't one of those arrogant assholes that be acting all extra. To be honest, he dressed like a broke dude. He had cars but preferred to be driven around, and there were many that were honored to play his chauffer.

The other guy that was helping him count and pack the money was his roommate, **ACE**. He was from the East Side. He was also corny looking. He didn't wear jewelry and didn't dress like a typical drug dealer who had money. He wore a shag and had a crazy curl. I don't know if it was a jeri or an S-curl. He rode a very nice motorcycle that sat outside their building. Neither of them was into flossing or showing off. If you really got it, you don't have to flaunt it. Right? I mean, why would you flaunt it? So a broke nigga can set you up for it? So the FEDS can get you? If you ever wondered how a lot of bosses have fallen, they fell victim to flossing. I heard a saying once, "Too much flossing can make your gums bleed." That metaphor is perfect. Let it marinate. Ace and Fritz were strictly about business.

Like I said, Tammy and I hung out down there a lot, but I never saw money in the house again after that first time. I guess they kept it somewhere else. That summer down on 112th Street was fun. It was all love. I met a lot of good guys down there. There were block parties and bus rides. Fritz even gave me and Tammy money to rent some buses for a free bus ride to Dorney Park. That's the type of guy he was.

I liked being around everybody down on 112th Street. The atmosphere down there was different. It was definitely a family oriented block. A lot of people would just be outside chillin', from old folks to babies. Fritz had a lot of love from a lot of people. He had a friend named Chuck who had a body better than Fifty Cent when he was at his peak. Chuck was thorough. He would have been the one that'll knock a dude out that didn't come correct. He always had pit bulls around him. Then there was Henry, a.k.a. Hen Dog. He was light skinned, dressed his ass off, fine as hell and he knew it too. My sister and I cracked the fuck up every time we saw him because he walked like he was on the runway. Henry was my dude. He was a real dude. Oh. I can't forget Al with his funny ass. He was cool too.

He loved to smoke. If it didn't have hash in it, he didn't want it. There were many others, but I would be remiss if I didn't mention Peggy. Peggy was one of a kind. She was a big woman, very loud and her presence was just huge. Her favorite word was "Bitch." I loved that woman. She took care of business for Ace and Fritz. It was one big family. You could feel the love and loyalty down there. Tammy and I could go to Fritz to get money anytime for anything. I couldn't believe it. I had been around money before, but this was different. These guys were money.

One day Fritz was like, "Somebody likes you."

I knew exactly who he was talking about so I just burst out laughing. It was his partner Ace. I wasn't too sure what to think about it though. I wasn't really interested for several reasons. The biggest reason was Lou. Mmmm Hmmm.

A few days after Fritz told me that, Tammy and I came down from his apartment and found Ace waiting for us on his motorcycle when we stepped out the building. I really didn't want to hurt his feelings so I gave him a few minutes of my time. I did think he was cute though. I didn't want to start anything I couldn't finish, but I loved money and he had it. We talked for a few minutes. He seemed cool so I gave him my beeper number and he gave me his.

He started calling and I must admit I found his conversation interesting. Those phone calls grew into him coming to my block to see me from time to time. He was real cool. He had one of the first cell phones. Do ya'll remember those shits? It was like holding a brick up to your face. It had a small antenna attached to it. Anyway, I told him I was a student at Bronx Community College and that I was having trouble paying my tuition. Back to my game being tight, I wasn't having trouble with shit. Financial Aid paid for everything. I ran game better than most niggas did. See while the average chick was into sneakers and bullshitting at 17, 18 and 19, I was into designer clothes, nice shoes and driving around. So I needed the money to support that lifestyle.

Shelli and I saw the bigger picture when we were young. We taught each other how to drive and got our license when we were like 15 and 16 years old. Not because we owned cars, because we didn't yet, but because there were too many dudes in the streets with cars and we wanted to drive them. Not knowing how to drive was always an excuse for them to say, "Nah ma, you can't drive." We were always thinking ahead.

Anyway, I wanted to see what Ace was working with, and it was a lot!!! I should've known by his name that he was about something. According to the dictionary, an Ace is someone with an exceptional skill, somebody who is outstanding at a particular activity. And that he was. Allegedly, that activity was selling a whole lot of crack and cocaine. He was caked up. You wouldn't think so by looking at him, but he was. He wore Dockers and t-shirts, making it obvious that clothes weren't his thing. Cars, money, motorcycles and making money were. I know I said money twice.

Ace and I talked about everything. He knew I had a man, but I guess he didn't care. It was like he needed someone to talk to more than anything else, and that was fine by me. He confessed that every time Tammy and I had left the apartment, he had watched me out the window with binoculars. I thought that was crazy, but hey whatever turned him on.

Look, let me give you an example of the kind of dude Ace was as well the kind of money they had. Fritz had gotten sick before we started talking, and Ace had a doctor flown in from the Islands to nurse him back to health with herbs and shit. Who does that? I thought about it and that sounded like money to me. I was very impressed with that. Ace is Caribbean himself. That showed me the love and loyalty he had for Fritz. That's what a real partner does. They had a serious bond. Ace had explained to me that he had a little trouble with the police on the East Side a while back, which is how he and Fritz became partners and roommates. He later revealed to me that he made his money on Madison Avenue and 129th Street. It was then that I figured out how some dudes in Harlem were getting money. That "how" was Ace and Fritz, and I knew both of them. No matter what, I knew Ace and I would be good friends.

He gave me the money to pay for school, which was actually used to go shopping. I bought Lou a few things too. First stop was Canal Street where I bought some big door knocker earrings and a diamond name chain. Canal Street used to be the spot to go buy bullshit jewelry. Everybody shopped there for jewelry. Although, back in the eighties and early nineties there was a Spanish dude on Broadway named Manny that everybody went to for the official diamonds. He was the Jacob the Jeweler of Harlem. Years later, I heard he was doing dumb shit like hooking dudes up with glass and fake diamonds instead of the real thing, allegedly. Shit, we didn't know the difference anyway.

Lou and I went shopping with the money Ace gave me. Don't judge me. He was a little suspicious about the money, but I said I got it from my mother. He didn't question it because my mother always looked out. Plus he knew my dad came back and forth from Jamaica with money. Then there was my uncle. So Lou really wouldn't have guessed another dude was in the picture. The best thing about Ace was that there was no sex involved. Unfortunately, there wasn't a lot of spending time involved either. He always apologized for being too busy to spend time with me and compensated that with money. That was fine with me because I didn't have the time either. It worked out great. I was happy. I just had to be careful. I was playing a very dangerous game, and I knew it.

One day Ace paged me and asked for my apartment number. I was like "Oh no, we can keep meeting outside, but the apartment is off limits." I thought he wanted the apartment number because he had already been to the building. He was like "Nah, I'm not coming to your house. I just need your address for something." I was a bit reluctant, but I gave it to him anyway. I knew one thing, if he and Lou ever bumped heads I was denying everything.

One day I came home from school and saw two dozen long stemmed roses on the dining room table. "Whose flowers are these?" I yelled to my mother.

"They're for you," she told me and handed me a little white card.

I was speechless. The roses were from Ace.

"Who are they from?" she asked.

I told her and shockingly she was very impressed. Shit I was impressed too. Then, as if he was somewhere watching me, my phone rang and it was him.

"You like your flowers?" He asked.

"Yes," I said with the biggest smile ever on my face.

He was definitely a keeper. I needed to make him mine. I didn't need to start a war though. I needed to think and fast. I couldn't let another bitch get this one. It was time for me to step my game up.

The delivery of roses came often. A month went by and Ace and I talked on the phone a lot. At the time he had a 4 year old son that he loved very much. He reluctantly told me that he had one on the way as well, but he and the mother weren't together. We often met up at places to talk, and each time he handed me a stack of cash before we parted ways. One day I went to Paragon and bought Lou a Marmot and some boots. It wasn't Fall yet, but we were starting early. SMH!!! I know ya'll dudes are like "Bitches ain't shit." Yeah, and neither are ya'll. LMAO.

Anyway, I had a good thing going until one day Lou asked, "Where the fuck you getting this money from?"

"Damn." I covered my face before replying, "Don't get mad." I said as I covered up.

Then I told him all about meeting a guy that was down with Fritz, but swore I wasn't fucking him and promised to stop taking his money. I thought Lou was going to kill me. Something like that was definitely grounds for an ass whipping, but he played it cool. I guess he realized that I spent some of that money on his ass too. Plus he knew I wasn't crazy enough to be having sex with someone else. I was really playing a very dangerous game. Something like that could've caused a major problem.

I kept in touch with Ace on the low. Ya'll gotta understand. I was young and somebody was giving me stacks of money just for talking. What chick wouldn't have taken that deal? The more I spoke to him the more I liked him. He was a simple person. He didn't really do much. Him and his boys would go hunting. Yes, hunting. He and his crew rode Upstate to the woods, camped out and hunted. He was definitely different. I didn't know Black men hunted. He was young too, around 23 at the time. Although the streets took up a lot of his time, his life seemed to be drama free. One day he invited me to a block party he threw on the East Side. It was packed. It was a back to school block party for the kids. He gave out backpacks filled with school supplies. I thought that was so nice of him. I guess it was only right he gave back to the community. I mean, the community was the reason he had all that money, if you know what I mean.

I wanted to get to know him better, but I couldn't. I needed to know who this dude from Madison Ave really was, and why was I just finding out about him? I was from the streets. I thought I knew about everybody. But you see, back then the West Side and the East Side stayed to themselves in a sense. Like I said before the East Side did their thing and the West Side did theirs, but it was still all love.

I really wanted to spend more time with Ace, but he was too busy anyway. I wondered what kind of street business would have a man running around all day. A million dollar Drug Empire, that's what.

R.I.P- Peggy, Chuck

Fritz and Chuck

I've Had Enough

One day I was feeling sick, wondering what the hell was going on. I found out I was pregnant. I was so in love with Lou that I didn't give a thought about those other children he had. I knew he loved me. I thought about all the good times we had and hoped the pregnancy would make things better. Yes I was talking to Ace, but Lou was my man. I was so sick. I had morning sickness all day. I was laid up in the bed or on the couch all day spitting and throwing up. It was disgusting. Then one night I got real bad cramps at like one in the morning.

Lou was Upstate with HER, but I still paged him because I couldn't bear the pain and I needed him. I decided to go to the hospital and my cousin Ronnie got in a cab with me. Sadly, it was too late. I miscarried in the cab. I was devastated. I got to Harlem Hospital and they gave me a D&C. I was just resting in my hospital bed when Lou got there that morning. I broke down crying and saw tears in his eyes too. I thought to myself, "Awww look at him, this man does have feelings." Seeing him like that was so sexy to me. That was my baby.

I later wondered if losing the baby was a sign. Maybe GOD knew that a baby wasn't the best choice for us at that time. I accepted the reality of the miscarriage. I just was going to enjoy the rest of my summer, so I thought.

One day my girls and I were on 8th Avenue in front of my building. We were just doing our usual, hanging on the corner. My girl Tia was talking to one of her dudes. Shelli and a few of the others were out there too. The Ave was packed with people. I was leaning up against a car next to Tia, who was talking to some guy on a pedal bike. I spotted Lou's car approaching and I smiled at the thought of seeing him. Then all of a sudden, the car pulled up really fast and screeched into a crazy ass U-turn, hitting me, Tia and the dude's bike. "BITCH!" I yelled out.

It was HER. Lou's baby mama from Upstate had just tried to kill me. I couldn't believe what happened. I had seen her before, but we never had any words. Everybody stopped, looking over at me in shock as the car sped off down the street. They didn't know what the fuck was going on, but I did. As the car sped off I knew just where she was going. I remembered Lou telling me she hung out downtown somewhere. I ran upstairs and got my pretty motherfucking .380 that Unique gave me and ran back downstairs. I paged Lou's ass with my 911 code about a hundred times. Then I called me a limo from Touch of Class cab service and me and all my girls piled up in that motherfucker on a mission.

While the limo was driving up and down 7th Avenue a car pulled up next to us. I swear I don't know how Lou's man Jay knew we were in there. He kept telling us to pull over. I begged the driver not to stop. I was scared as shit. I don't know where Lou was, but I knew he was close and we were not stopping. I screamed at the driver to take me to the precinct. He dropped me off in front of the 32nd precinct. He then took my girls back to the block. Next thing I knew his man Jay drove by slowly and Lou came walking up to the precinct from 8th Avenue. This MF came straight to the precinct. He didn't care that there was a hundred police nearby. He smiled and said, "Come on." And my ass went with him. Ughhh. He made me sick. LOL.

I'm sure SHE had an ass whipping waiting on her for that stunt she pulled.

****

If that shit with Lou's baby mama wasn't enough, it wasn't long before I caught his ass cheating again. I had suspected he was cheating with this chick that my uncle had messed with. She was a big freak. Anyway, I was pissed so of course I called my partner in crime, Shelli. I paged Lou and had him come to my building. He was sitting in his car with his windows rolled down while Shelli and I stood on the curb. I started screaming on him and then pulled my gun out. It wasn't my .380 either. This time it was an old, long ass gun my cousin's father had from one of those fucking wars. LMAO.

Lou just sat there with a wicked smile and shook his head.

"Tee, don't let me get out this car," he warned.

I continued cursing, yelling and poppin' shit like I do.

"Yo Shelli," he told my cousin. "You better get her."

Shelli jumped in front of me and leaned on the door so he couldn't get to me.

"Run, Tee run," she yelled.

Until this day, Shelli and I still crack the fuck up about that night. We had some crazy ass times. I still should've shot him right in his ass. LOL.

After that I started distancing myself from Lou. I started acting funny and he felt it. I was really sick of his shit. The more Lou thought he was slick, the closer I got to stepping my game up. I needed to get away from that drama. Bitches were trying to kill me and this dude was still acting up. Okay MF. I started paging Ace again. All that "corny", was becoming more and more attractive.

Lou didn't know what was going on with me. I'm sure he knew that his actions were definitely the reason for my distance. I played it cool though. I told him that I didn't feel like being bothered and I needed some space. He asked why and I told him that I was slacking in school.

"Okay," he said with a nod, but there was a look in his eyes I would never forget. I know he didn't believe me. It was like he saw right through me. He had other bitches he needed to deal with anyway. I knew he loved me, but I had to do me. Why not? He was doing him.

Although I loved Lou, I had to do what I felt was right for me. In addition to distancing myself from him, I distanced myself from Stan too. I mean, I couldn't go but so far, but still. It was just that something was always going on; a shooting here, a shooting there. They blaming shit on Lou or somebody's trying to kill Stan. Then I got phone calls threatening my life. WTF!!! The year wasn't even over yet and so much had already gone down.

I knew Lou had nothing to do with all the drama that was going on in the streets, but it was hard for him to remove his name from all that was going on while dudes in his own crew were doing dumb shit making matters worse. Fat Boy tried to get them to stop, but the damage was done. Anything that happened was blamed on one person, Lou. He was getting deeper and deeper into shit in the streets. I was afraid he might get hurt in the streets and that was something I just couldn't handle. Shit was getting hectic and I didn't know what to expect. On top of all that, I was also afraid for my own well-being. What if someone came after him while we were together? I was confused and didn't know what to do. Then of course there was the baby mama drama and the bitches. I just had enough. Love or lust just isn't enough reason to stay when everything else is all wrong. I made my decision and my mind was made up.

A few weeks went by with little to know contact between me and Lou. Then I saw him one day hanging out with some guys across the street from my building. I was walking home with a handful of shopping bags from Macy's, The Gap, and Benetton. I felt the tension from across the street and saw the anger in his eyes.

"Damn. Does he know about me and Ace?" I thought.

I didn't know what to do. I took off to my building as fast as I could, but the lobby door was locked and he was on my ass. I hurried through the first set of lobby doors and he rushed in behind me. Without a word, he punched me in the face, threw me to the ground, and snatched my diamond chain off my neck. There were two security guards around too. He looked at them and again walked out like no one could do him any harm.

"Some fucking security," I screamed.

That was the second time security let me get fucked up in that building. "Why did he do that?" I wondered as I struggled upstairs into my apartment with my bags. Even more, I was pissed that no one came to my rescue. I spent that whole night on the phone trying to get him to give me my chain back. Even my mother and crazy ass aunt asked him about what he did to me, and he told a big ass lie that he didn't do it. And he lied to the GOD, aka my mother. Hell NAW!! Okay MF. The truth was, I really didn't need to beg for it. I had enough money to go buy five more chains if I wanted to, but one was enough. So the first thing the next morning, I took some money I got from Ace and ordered another one.

After that incident I knew then it was over for real, and so did Lou. I needed more than just space. It was time to leave, but where would I go? Who could I run to? It had to be with someone

Lou couldn't or wouldn't try to touch? On the streets, power respects power. It had nothing to do with being a punk or being scared because anybody could get it at any time. Whoever I ran to had to be strong, powerful and well respected.

Little did I know I was already where I needed to be. So, into Ace's arms I ran. Lou didn't know him personally, but once you say 112th or Fritz there was no more to be said. Fritz was powerful and anybody around him was well respected. Plus a lot of niggas ate because of 112th Street. Lou by no means was scared of anybody, but he respected their gangsta and they respected his. I guess he respected my wishes to go elsewhere too. I know he didn't like it, but he respected it.

A New Start

I didn't love Ace, but I had to go somewhere else. I figured I could learn to love him. I knew he didn't love me either, but he liked me a lot and that was enough. He accepted me into his life with no problems. He was sweet and kind and ready to do whatever to make me happy.

When we got together he took me to two apartments that he said we would share together. One was uptown on 151st Street and Convent and the other was a building on the East Side called 1199. They were both fully furnished. We had two cars, a customized van and he had his motorcycle. We also had a private driver from Touch of Class car service, who was on call 24 hours a day and only worked for Ace. The driver got paid whether Ace used him or not. His name was 23.

Ace also had two pit-bulls that had their own apartment in a brownstone on 119th and Lenox Ave. That was crazy because I knew some dudes that didn't even have their own apartment. I know some guys today that don't have their own shit. SMH!!! Anyway, I moved into the apartment on Convent. It was next door to the 30th precinct, so I felt safe until I heard about the dirty thirty. They say that precinct was so corrupt it was a shame.

Ace spent a lot of time at a house in Long Island that he and Fritz chilled at with Big Dee and her chick. Yeah, Big Dee was a woman and she liked chicks. I couldn't believe I was starting a new life with this dude. Just like that, it was over between me and Lou and I was with Ace. Little did I know, this fantasy would be short-lived.

You have to understand. I had been dealing with dudes from the streets since I was 15. Back then it was exciting having a boyfriend in the streets wreaking havoc, selling dope and making tons of money. Back then a dude could afford to support a wifey plus a few chicks on the side. Trickin' was the thing to do. The drug game was big business, and chicks were gettin' a piece of the game in one way or another. Big Dee dove into the game to get her piece too. She was a hustler from Madison Ave. She had the projects on Madison Ave on lock. Those were the same projects Maine was from. She was the truth. She had a crew of lil niggas that was definitely bringing that paper in. I use to see her on 7th Ave talking to Rich Porter and AZ. She was a part of the family from 112th. It was like the black mob, *La familia*, except there wasn't too much focus if any on murders. It was all about gettin' money.

Big Dee and her girl had an apartment in our building uptown too. The building was brand new. We lived on the same floor. Her girl lived with her; well one of her girls lived with her. She liked them chicks and she had plenty of 'em. You know what they say, "Money talks." Her chicks were cute and fly. One time, two of her girls got into a fight over her in front of the building. It was the craziest shit I ever saw. Funny as hell too.

My new situation was alright though. I wanted for nothing. The Convent Ave apartment was perfect for me. Although the apartment downtown was bigger with two bedrooms and a terrace, I liked the smaller apartment better. We were on a high floor and I was scared of the terrace. Anyway, Ace showed me some money in a drawer. It was like $30,000 that was only to be used for an emergency, but of course I dipped in it here and there. Like if a special occasion came up, like a birthday or Christmas, I was able to buy my family nice things. He gave me the keys to both cars. At the time Acura Legends were hot. It was champagne colored just like Shelli's, but mine had an indented trunk. Do ya'll remember indented trunk? Carlos from the Auto Clinic hooked it up. I also had a black 325 BMW. It had black leather seats with white piping. But it was stick shift so I couldn't drive it.

Ya'll ain't gonna believe this shit but, we had a hawk too. A goddamn hawk that had its own apartment on 112th Street. Now a hawk was and still is an endangered species. Right? I didn't know Black men hunted and I didn't know Black men or any man had pet hawks. I know ya'll like that dude was weird, but he wasn't. He was just different. Ace fed the hawk pigeons. He was the only one that actually entered that apartment because I think that MF would peck the shit out of you and kill you. Everybody else that fed it opened the door and tossed in a few pigeons before slamming the door back.

At twenty-one, I thought I was doing pretty good for myself. Any chick would've loved to have been in my position at that time. I had everything a girl wanted and needed. My only complaint was not seeing Ace as much as I wanted to. He was really busy. He must've been selling a lot of drugs. One thing I can say for sure is that I never saw drugs in our house. That's a mistake a lot of dudes made back then too. Home should be home. Sometimes Ace left the house at nine in the morning and returned at two, three or four the next morning. He was gone at least 19 hours a day. I wondered if he was cheating or had another girl on the side, or if I was the girl on the side. It really didn't matter because I had the cars, access to the money and I had the keys to the apartments. I wasn't going anywhere and neither was he.

I thought that was the life. Back then, a lot of young girls in the hood aspired to end up with a drug dealer with a lot of money and a nice car. It wasn't a good way of thinking. To find someone with a good and decent job wasn't even a thought. That's not what we were looking for anyway. We wanted fast money. We weren't thinking about corporate professionals. The only Black men with good jobs were actors and ball players, so we thought. The rappers weren't even making money back then. I wanted a drug dealer. We all wanted one. If any chick from Harlem says she didn't, she's lying. Things aren't always what they seemed though.

My dad use to always say in his thick Jamaican accent, "Ms. Tee, money is the root to all evil."

I really didn't think about what that meant. Back then I didn't see the bigger picture. I soon found out that money really was the root to all evil. There was always someone lurking out there who wanted what you had and was ready and willing to get it by any means necessary. It wouldn't be long before I found out how right my father was.

****

In The Fall of 1990, I found out I was pregnant. At first I had doubts about keeping it because I wasn't in love with Ace, but I did love him. He was in love with me and was able to provide everything the baby and I needed so it didn't take long for me to convince myself. Although Ace and I hadn't been together that long, I decided to keep it. If anybody was ready to take care of a baby it was him. Yeah, I know you're saying, "Why didn't she just enjoy the moment?" Why complicate shit with a baby, right? Fuck that. LOL. Nah, my answer is I don't know. All I knew back then was I was keeping that one. My situation was different back then. Even if he decided to leave me, I was already set up. I had an apartment, I mean two apartments, money, cars and I knew he would take care of his child. Maybe that's why I didn't just enjoy the moment. Maybe I wanted more than just a moment with Ace.

I was never a female that thought a baby could keep a man. I'd been to the clinic before, if you know what I mean. I loved money and was too selfish to share it with a baby. A baby was always the furthest thing from my mind. I wasn't trying to keep them MF's back then anyway. LMAO. But fo' real, if a man wants you then he'll keep you, with or without a baby. A lot of women and young girls get the game twisted. These niggas don't give a fuck about no baby, especially if he's not feeling you. Never do it because he has money, because that's just what it is, his money. Not yours. See I knew I had Ace. I never had a problem keeping a man anyway. You have to make sure that man wants, loves and respects you. Make sure he just doesn't have you to pass the time until someone else comes along. And never be a rebound chick.

Ace already had two sons, but now he would have three kids. Big Dee told me about one of his baby mamas from the East Side he was with for a long time. I don't know how, but I got this girl's phone number and it was on. My friends and I phone harassed her like crazy. I guess I wanted to make sure that she was never coming back. The thought of him and someone else made me crazy. Maybe I was falling in love. I was just young and crazy. Eventually, I just had to deal with the fact that there were others before me and there would be other children besides mine. That's one of the things you have to expect when dealing with a dude in the streets. I had to charge it to the game. Our kids eventually ended up growing close and loving each other as brother and sister. SHE and I are real cool too. "Hey Girl."

After the news of the pregnancy, Ace proposed. He gave me a beautiful diamond ring that had stones going down one side of the ring and a nice sized diamond in the middle. He also gave me a full length Blue Fox fur coat that Christmas. I guess he wanted me to know that he loved me and that I was the only thing that mattered to him.

****

One morning Fritz came to our house. I was surprised because he rarely came uptown. As a matter of fact that was the only time he came to the house. I went in the room, but I heard him saying that Henry's brother and girlfriend had been arrested at one of the apartments downtown. It was a big case that made the news. They made them an offer, but they decided to go to trial. Henry's brother was a good dude that was very smart. He went to an Ivy League school. He just happened to be at the wrong place at the wrong time. It was sad because Henry didn't want to see his family go down that way. He was crushed. We all were. That wasn't even his brother's life. Eventually he blew trial and never gave anybody up. They gave him 15 years to life. I guess the jury believed that with that amount of drugs that were found in the apartment, he had to be involved.

****

Lou had stopped speaking to me when I got with Ace. I missed him a lot. I still loved him, but I didn't have time for all that drama that came with being his girl. I hardly saw him. I tried my best to avoid seeing him anyway. I was living uptown and spent my time driving around with my girls having fun and playing the housewife for Ace. Fat Boy and I were still cool though. I always kept my ears to the streets. Lou's name was still ringing bells out there. I had heard that another one of his friends got killed. It seemed like all his friends were dying. It would've killed me if someone tried to hurt him. I say tried because I knew they would've had a hard time doing it.

I bumped into Fat Boy one day and he told me that Lou was okay. I wanted the best for Lou, but only he could make things better for himself. I was glad I had Fat Boy and Lou's man Beatty to keep me up on what was going on with him. They were really like my brothers.

Ace

Paid In Full

The directors who made the movie Paid in Full told their version of the events surrounding the murder and kidnapping of Rich Porter and his younger brother the best way they knew how. What they didn't tell you was how Rich tried to get the money to get his brother back. Well, guess what? I can fill in that part of the story because the money came from my people. And when I say my people, I'm talking about Fritz and Ace.

As you can see a lot of shit went down in 1990. One day Ace and I had a conversation about Rich Porter, which was one of the worst things that had taken Harlem by storm and that was when Rich Porter's little brother Darnell was kidnapped in December of 1989. I can't even begin to imagine what Rich was going through, but then again I can because I love my daughter so much that the mere thought of anything or anyone hurting her makes me lose my mind. But if Darnell's kidnapping wasn't crazy enough, the unthinkable happened in January 1990. Rich Porter was killed and they found him and his brother's bodies. Although it's been 25 years, a loss is a loss. Time doesn't take away the pain; it just makes life a little easier to live.

Anyway, I had a conversation with Ace and this is how he told me it went down.

According to Ace, Rich called up Fritz one night and Ace and Fritz met him downtown on 99th Street and 5th Avenue. Of course Rich told Fritz about his brother's kidnapping and the ransom request. Rich was devastated and scared for his brother's safety. Fritz assured Rich that he would do anything to help him get his brother back. Rich and Fritz met up in person a few more times after that initial meeting, but Fritz eventually stopped meeting up with Rich because he knew the FEDS were following Rich.

One day Rich made a mistake of calling Fritz from his mother's apartment, which was tapped by the FEDS. The FEDS showed up to Fritz' house the same day, but the man who answered the door told them that Fritz had left five minutes earlier. What the FEDS didn't know was that it was Fritz who had answered the door. Once they left, Fritz left his building on 107th Street and Madison Ave out of a side door. The FEDS were outside waiting and they obviously had no clue who the hell they were looking for.

Before all this went down, Rich had Ace confused with Henry. You'll learn all about Henry later. Rich always thought Henry was Ace, and Henry never corrected him. I guess Henry had the look and style that people thought someone like Ace would have. Like I said, although Ace and Fritz were two of the richest dudes in Harlem, but they damn sure didn't look like your average drug dealers. It wasn't until shortly before the whole kidnapping thing that Fritz and Ace went to meet Rich on 131st & 7th Avenue one day and they were introduced. Rich said he heard a lot about Ace from talk on the streets. See what I'm saying? The streets be talking too much.

But back to Fritz helping Rich with the ransom. Ace can't remember how much cash Fritz gave Rich, but he's certain that Fritz gave him 30 kilos of cocaine to pay the ransom. Fritz gave the coke to Rich at a price of $23k a kilo. That totaled $690,000, which covered the ransom that the kidnappers were asking for in full. Because the FEDS were going to be investigating Rich when the ordeal was over, Fritz sent him some cash as well to help him leave town or just chill if he wanted to. Fritz also suggested that Rich just fall back altogether.

Of course Rich couldn't sell the 30 bricks himself because he was being watched by the FEDS. It's strongly alleged that he gave the 30 bricks to Alpo to sell. This is where you'll learn that money is the root to all evil ya'll. Alpo allowed greed to consume him and took advantage of the opportunity presented, which was Darnell's kidnapping. He figured that the perfect time to kill Rich was while Rich was out trying to get his brother back. It would make it look like the same people that kidnapped Darnell did it. It's fucked up that Alpo took advantage of that opportunity. What type of motherfucker would do something so cruel to someone at a time like that? Ya'll feel me? SMH!!!

After Rich was killed, Alpo allegedly went looking for Rich's lieutenant. Before I go on let me explain what a lieutenant is to those who don't know. Every major drug gang, cartel, crew or whatever you want to call it has a lieutenant. The lieutenant is the boss' right hand man. Maine had a lieutenant too, but his happened to be a female. Stan and Al had lieutenants. Lieutenants are for those crews that are getting major money and running a 24 hour business, not those bum ass dudes and crews I described earlier. You know the one's hustling for nothing. Got it? Anyway, at the time Rich was killed, his lieutenant was the only one who knew that Rich gave Alpo the 30 bricks, so of course he had to go. The lieutenant ended up getting to Fritz and telling him that Alpo had those bricks for sure. That dude ended up dead. My cousin Shelli use to mess with that lieutenant, but I'm not going to say his name because he might be a victim in an unsolved murder case, if you get what I'm saying?

Fritz set up a meeting with Alpo in Big Dee's store over on 132nd Street & Madison Ave. Alpo pulled up in a few Lincoln Town cars with some dudes believed to be from D.C. He stepped in and flashed two guns at Fritz to let him know he came prepared, but he had no idea that Fritz had a gun aimed at him and those cars he pulled up with the entire time. Shit, who wouldn't have taken those precautions? For a nigga like Alpo, you needed motherfuckers across the street on rooftops aiming guns at every door of every car he rolled up with to make sure he didn't make it out of there alive. I'm just saying. Just in case something goes south, you gotta be prepared. Fritz was ready so it would've gotten real crazy if it did jump off.

Fritz asked Alpo about the 30 kilos of coke and this nigga said, "a dead man can't pay." You'll see later that niggas started to run with that phrase. He was basically saying "Yeah I got them, but you gave them to Rich and he's gone."

All along, Fritz thought that Alpo would do the right thing because Alpo was Rich's man. Fritz was thinking that maybe he and Alpo could do business together, but at that time he had no idea that Alpo was the one that killed Rich. Ain't that some shit? If Alpo would've done the right thing, Fritz was prepared to give him 100 bricks to rock with.

After the meeting, Ace felt some type of way about what Alpo said and wanted to take care of him, if you know what I mean, but Fritz said no. That's what I was talking about when I said you can't mix murder and the drug business. Fritz had an empire and he couldn't afford to lose it. A lot of dudes couldn't afford to lose 30 bricks and would've been forced to put murder into the mix in that situation, but Fritz was on a different level. I'm not saying Fritz could afford to just throw 30 bricks away, but 30 bricks was not worth losing an empire over.

We all know how that story ended. Alpo confessed to killing Rich and went to jail. So, what do you think about that shit? He was dead wrong for killing Rich, and especially at the time he did it. How can anyone put a mother through some shit like that? That was Harlem for ya. That money drove motherfuckers insane. Oh yeah, and Alpo may be back in Harlem soon. Let's see how many of ya'll niggas jump on his dick. LMMFAO!!! I'm just saying. Don't be mad because a bitch is speaking the truth. I know some of ya'll are a little nervous, but I don't blame ya'll. He might not kill you, but Po will fuck you up. I know for a fact he's good with those hands. I personally saw him knock somebody out. Although that was a long time ago, I'm sure he's still got it.

Po, I'm just a story teller, so don't be mad at me. By the way, can I hold something. LOL.

I know it's not gonna happen, but it would be nice if I could get paid in full from some of those loser ass fools that still owe Ace hundreds of thousands of dollars. Let's be clear, owing a MF never ends. But as ya'll know, that's how that street thing goes. People forget the one who helped them feed their families, pay their bills and allowed them to be tricks to those bum ass chicks they were fucking out there. LMAO. But hey, what else can I say.

Reality Hits Home

1991 had to be the best and worst year ever for me. It was February and I was three months pregnant. Everything was going so good for me and Ace, and then the unthinkable happened. I got a call saying that Ace got arrested on the East Side.

"They say it's for some murder that happened back in '87," Ace told me when he was finally able to call.

"What they mean four years ago?"

I couldn't believe that shit was happening. I mean, they got him for some shit that allegedly happened four years earlier. What took them so long to get him? It wasn't like he was hiding. It was some real bullshit to me. First Henry's people and now Ace. Fritz was very upset, but I knew he would make everything alright.

"Everything will be okay," I kept telling myself.

Ace said he had no idea what they were talking about. He said he didn't do it. We found out that the witness was some crack head prostitute from the East Side. "Who the fuck is going to believe her?" I thought. I was sure it had to be a mistake or a set up.

Ace had me take $25K to his lawyer to start the case. He was arraigned on February 25th. I remember that shit like it was yesterday. The judge denied him bail. We even offered to put up a million dollars in cash or collateral to bail him out, but the judge still denied him bail. He ended up getting indicted for murder. I couldn't believe what was happening. Was I going to have this baby alone? What about the rents? What about everything? I was only 21 years old and I felt like I had the weight of the world on my shoulders.

Over the next few weeks, I visited Ace every chance I got and we talked on the phone every day. In March, we hired a private investigator to see what was up with that witness. Although we talked a lot about how to handle his case, the majority of those visits and phone calls consisted of long talks about his business and what he needed to be done. I was responsible for handling his business, which meant I was back in the drug game. I picked up in the streets where Ace left off. I didn't have to, but I wanted to. Plus, wasn't nobody fuckin' my money up. If niggas owed Ace, they owed me and my baby. I was ready for all the bullshit too. You know, niggas think the boss is off the scene and start getting stupid. The next thing you know they trying to play the next in line with stupid ass stories. The "I got robbed" stories. The "My baby mama called the police" bullshit. The "We got raided" tale. Dudes are a trip. But I was having none of that.

Ace left a lot of money in the streets, and he gave me the names of everybody that owed. From the East Side to the West Side and from downtown to uptown, dudes owed this man money. There were two dudes on the East Side that owed around $25K and the other owed about $50K. There was a dude from uptown that owed about $62K. So there was enough money out there for me to survive. Now remember, I was only 21 years old at the time, but I'll tell ya'll this though, I was moving like a Boss Bitch when I made my rounds to pick that money up. Yeah, they were looking at me crazy. Some had the sob stories. And some gave that money up because they really didn't know what was going on with Ace's case. They wanted to be on good terms with him just in case he happened to come home sooner rather than later. There were a few that ran that "come back tomorrow" shit on me. If I really wanted to, I could've gotten every penny from all those fools. I mean, all I had to do was go to 142nd Street or make a phone call to you know who, but I wasn't ready to mix those two worlds just yet.

Fritz called me up and told me to buy a safe. Of course I took his advice. I purchased a heavy duty safe from Trevor locksmith over on 127th and 7th Avenue. That thing was so heavy that even though it rolled we still had to damn near get on our hands and knees to push it. A fire wouldn't have destroyed that thing. Fritz promised that Ace would still get his share of whatever money came through their partnership. That's what REAL MEN do. That's love, a true friendship and what being a real business partner is about. That's what LOYALTY is about fellas. Not too many dudes are built like Fritz. They don't make 'em like they used to. Nowadays, once a dude is gone and locked up, it's more money for the next man. Some of ya'll dudes are just greedy. Ya'll want all the money, even if it means crossing your man to get it. Then ya'll try to fuck ya man's girl while he's away. Ya'll know that selfish shit I'm talking about. Trifling ass motherfuckers.

Fritz not only gave me money to put away, he also paid my bills. And I still had pocket money from what Ace had left in the house. THANK GOD.

Ace spent the next few months going back and forth to court for hearings, motions, and this and that. All that shit gave me a headache. His lawyer, Levine, was constantly filing paperwork, doing whatever he could to dismiss the charges. After a few court appearances, the DA started throwing offers around. One was a 6 to 18 year bid. Ace seriously considered that offer, but Fritz was like, "Hell No! If you didn't do it don't cop out. Never plead guilty to something you didn't do." It made sense at the time.

I'm pregnant and sick as a dog, throwing up and spitting all over the goddamn place. I was a mess. I was running back and forth to Rikers Island. It was crazy. I made sure Ace had whatever he needed. I also made sure his wardrobe was up. Ya'll didn't forget how I told ya'll this nigga dressed, did ya'll? Dockers and shit. Nah, that wasn't working on the Island. I needed to make sure he was right over there. I had to Americanize his ass. It had to be clear, "Yeah ya'll, this that nigga from downtown that got that change." LMAO. I couldn't have my baby daddy over there looking crazy. No Sir.

Ace called one day and told me that Henry told him that he thought Fritz was getting sick again, but was refusing to go to the hospital. Ace didn't like that. With Ace away, there was only one dude downtown that would be in charge if anything happened to Fritz, and Ace wasn't feeling this dude because he wasn't taking care of The King like he was supposed to. Ya'll know how it is. It's always a MF that wants to be that nigga so bad and thinks he could do things better, but he had it ALL fucked up. I told ya'll earlier, everybody's not meant to be a boss. I guess this dude was too focused on all the moves he hoped to make when he got his chance instead of taking care of the boss that was making all the moves happen at the moment. Nobody was supposed to think like that when it came to The King. Everybody was supposed to make sure

The King is good and gets whatever help necessary, by all and any means necessary.

Let me break this down real quick before I get to the next bullshit that happened to me. When you're down with someone that is (for a lack of a better word) THAT NIGGA, you're supposed to make sure he's good. When THAT NIGGA is the one that keeps money in your pocket and will put in that work for you and the block, you're supposed to make sure he's good. I say all this to say, everybody's not built to be THAT NIGGA. Just because you wanna be, don't mean you have the ability to be. Everyone has a part to play and a lane to stay in. And that's that.

Damn, Why They Wanna Stick Me For My Paper?

I was starting to get a little worried about Fritz. I prayed that he would be okay. Ace wasn't there so there was no way Fritz could get sick on me. I needed him. Everything was running smooth. The business had been going well with minor setbacks here and there. Every now and then somebody fucked up, but there was nothing major. I was sick and in the house a lot so I would let Ace's workers hold my car. And what they do? Get a bunch of tickets and didn't pay them. It was always something. They were all young and immature.

I kept that safe I bought at my mother's house. The main reason for that was because I didn't want anybody knowing where I lived. The only person that ever came to me and Ace's apartment was Fritz, and I was going to keep it that way. Another reason was because I was sick and wanted to be around family. I kept a ledger of everybody I did business with. I kept that locked away in the safe. As far as business was concerned, I had a nice routine set up. Ace's crew came to my mom's house to drop off money and pick up product. They were basically still finishing off the work Ace had before he got locked up. I had two kilos of cocaine and a big garbage bag full of weed. The weed wasn't for sale. That was Ace personal weed. Yep a garbage bag full. SMH! Once the coke was sold I would've been done. I would've just been saving whatever money I got from Fritz and off the streets.

Most of this dropping off and picking up was done while my mother was at work and of course my pops was in Jamaica. Hustling wasn't new to me so I did what I had to do. I had kilos to sell and a crew of lil niggas to babysit. Aces' crew already knew what to do. His crew was the only ones allowed in the house because they were the crew. You should be able to trust your crew, right? And the crew is the backbone of the business, right?

I needed to get rid of those two kilos of cocaine so I called Hen one day and asked him to find somebody to take them off my hands. He said "Okay," and ended up calling me right back and said he'll take them. We met up at around eight that night, and since he was family, I sold him both kilos for seventeen thousand five hundred a piece. That price was good at the time. I think it was around one of those drought times too, so I know he made a killing off that shit. Some of us remember those days and weeks when it was a drought. One major drug bust somewhere can slow everything down and send the price of cocaine and heroin through the roof.

Well, a few days after I sold the two kilos to Hen, someone from Aces' crew stopped by to pick up some money to take to Aces' dad, who was sick. Soon after he left with the money, there was a knock on the door. I thought it was Lil Sis because I told her to come home at a certain time. I walked to the door in my bra and panties with my big belly sticking out. I barely said "Who…" when a girl's voice called my name. I figured it was my sister and snatched the door open without checking the peephole. WRONG MOVE!!

Three individuals rushed in wearing black masks, carrying a Tech 9, a Mac 11 and a 9mm. I'll tell ya'll later how I found out what kind of guns they had. Anyway, it was two dudes and a fucking female. I couldn't believe it. All I thought about was "these motherfuckers are playing me." They closed the door and pushed me to the floor while aiming their guns at my face and head. I fought and knocked the barrels of their guns away from my direction. I was scared that one of the guns might mistakenly go off, and I didn't want it pointed at me if it did.

The bitch called my name like she knew me and said, "Don't worry Tonia, you'll be okay. Just take us to the safe."

"Safe? How the fuck they know I got a safe in here?" I thought. That's when I knew I'd been set the fuck up. Ya'll might not believe me, but at first I wasn't even scared. All I kept thinking was, "If I make it out of this, it's on when I find out who's responsible for this shit. I'm putting cash money on a nigga's head for this shit." I think I was in shock and that's the reason why I wasn't nervous or scared. I couldn't wrap my head around the idea that somebody was doing that to me. They took me to the back where I kept the safe.

They knew exactly where to take me.

"Open it," one of the dudes barked, pushing me to my knees in front of the safe.

I acted like I was too nervous to open it.

The same dude said, "I'm going to kill her."

I turned to them and snapped, "I'll be a dead rich bitch up in here and won't open up shit."

I was acting real brave and talking a lot of shit. I guess I felt I had more power than they did at that time. Fo' real tho, I was buggin' for saying any of that shit. They could have really did me dirty.

"You'll be okay. Just open the safe," the bitch said while reaching over my shoulder and taking my engagement ring off my finger.

"Hell no," I muttered. "This nigga talking reckless and I'm not opening up shit." There I go again with the bullshit. No lie.

I was surprised at myself for talking shit to them, but I did have the upper hand. They wanted what I had. The other dude commenced to taking the rest of my jewelry off the dresser and putting it in a knapsack. The ball was in my hands because the safe was too heavy for them to carry and they needed to get out of there quick. I realized they were starting to get antsy, and the seriousness of the situation hit me. So what did I do? I went into survival mode.

"Look," I pleaded. "Please don't hurt me and my baby. I'll open the safe then you can tie me up and leave me here." Yes I told them to tie me up. I just wanted to assure them that I wasn't on no bullshit and I just wanted them gone.

The bitch nodded at her partners. "Okay," she said.

I took a real chance trusting them to keep their word about tying me up and leaving me behind, alive. I don't suggest anyone else try that if they find themselves in the same position. You have to do what works for you. I opened the safe and then the same dude that threatened to kill me screamed, "Get on the bed and put a pillow over your head."

"That nigga must watch too much T.V." I thought. "Hell no!" I yelled. "You better tie my ass up and leave me here like we said. I'm not putting no pillow over my head."

He snatched the telephone wire out the wall and tied me up with it.

"Please take the money and go," I told them.

They took the jewelry, the bag of weed, and over a hundred fifty grand in cash. But you know what had me more concerned than any of that? That ledger. It had names, dates, and phone numbers of everybody I did business with and everybody that owed us money. I didn't want it to somehow fall into the hands of the police. Not to mention those stupid ass robbers could've went after everybody in that book. That's what scared me. Fuck money. Money comes and goes. That book was worth more than the money that just ran out the door. That book could've cost lives. I was pissed they took my engagement ring too. And I was mad at Fritz for making me get that bad luck ass safe. It felt like my world was crumbling down. I couldn't breathe. I felt faint. I was supposed to take the money uptown to my apartment. I usually took some every couple of days just in case. I got lazy and missed a couple of days, or maybe even weeks.

A million thoughts ran through my mind in an instant. What did I do? Was GOD punishing me? Was I being punished for putting money before love and doing the right thing? What was the right thing? I didn't know what to do or what to think. I heard my daddy's voice in my ear, "Ms. Tee, money is the root to all evil." I wish that crazy ass Jamaican was in town at the time. Trust me somebody would've been left behind. Keith played no games. He kept a ratchet knife or a gun on him.

Those fools didn't even tie me up tight. I waited until they were out the house and took the wire off my wrist before throwing some clothes on and running to the front door. My sister was standing there when I opened it.

"I just got robbed. Take the steps," I told her.

We got to the first floor and saw hoodies and black masks lying on the stairwell floor. They were gone. My sister and I stepped out the building and I fell to the ground. Right then and there is when it all hit me. Some of my friends that were out there ran over to me. I got up and went back into the building. The security guard said that three people left the building in a hurry and it looked like they were sweating. REALLY MF? I couldn't even call the cops. What would I tell them? "They just robbed me for my drug money." It was like a movie or a dream and I hoped to see the credits rolling or wake up soon. But I didn't, because it wasn't a movie or a dream. I went back to the stairwell and grabbed the clothes they left behind. I put those clothes in a plastic bag and tossed it in the safe. Don't ask me why. There was a part of me that thought I could use that as evidence to find who did it.

I knew just who had something to do with it and he was going to be dealt with accordingly. That MF had left my house just before I got that knock at the door. He didn't even know how to set a motherfucker up right. Or did he expect them to kill me? He was jealous that Ace left me with the responsibility of taking care of the business. He felt that responsibility should've been given to him. Fuck that, it's my man, our money and that's that. I was mad, but I was okay because I could always get money. Plus I had a nice little nest egg uptown. I couldn't spend it though. That was all I had.

I tried to analyze what happened. I wasn't really mad at the robbers at all. It was the MF that sent them that needed to be disciplined. They were just doing what they were told. Whoever robbed me had to split that money up and they would probably blow right through it. They weren't hustlers so I knew they would be out of money real soon trying to rob somebody else. I was certain that one day I would find out just what happened. I knew who set me up. I just needed confirmation. But confirmation or not, I told Ace that I was going to have dude killed if and when I found him, and I meant it. There was absolutely nothing Ace could've said that would've made me change my mind.

I remember thinking, "Damn, I wish Maine was here." He was away doing a bid at the time. One thing I can say for sure is that things would've gotten ugly if he was home. He would have made sure I was okay.

I called Fritz and we got together to talk about what had happened. He pulled up in the back seat of a BMW at around nine the next night with a dude I didn't recognize behind the wheel. I hopped in the back seat with him and instantly noticed he wasn't feeling well. His beard was getting longer and he refused to cut it. It was May and he had a light scarf around his neck. He wasn't too comforting either, but when The King talked you listened. He seemed a little disoriented. He was talking gibberish that didn't make much sense at the time.

He pointed at my building and said, "Whoever was involved came from in there. You know them."

"Really?" I thought to myself. I just didn't have time for crazy talk.

I thought it was the sickness invading his brain. Little did I know, what he was saying would be right. I just sat there and listened to him. I loved Fritz and it hurt me to see him like that. It was like he was going through it alone too because nobody downtown seemed like they cared. Henry cared and some others, but the main motherfucker that should've made sure Fritz saw a doctor was just watching him rot away. I wished Ace was there to take care of him. I felt bad about his situation, but I had my own shit to deal with.

GOD works in mysterious ways. Remember I said that I had told my sister to come home at a certain time on the night that I got robbed? Well she did come upstairs, but she stopped to talk to my best friend April's little brother when she got off the elevator. She was 15 at the time. Anybody that knows her knows she's a fighter. Lil Sis use to get busy with chicks. Anyway, I KNOW for a fact that if she was in that house, things would've turned out differently. Her mind would've been telling her that we weren't going to get out of there alive and her gut instinct would've made her fight her way out. When the robbers left and were running down the hall, my sister heard footsteps followed by the stairwell door closing. Her and the guy she was talking to looked around the corner, but didn't see anything. Had she ended that conversation a minute sooner, she would've bumped into them coming out the apartment or ended up in the apartment while it was going down. That's crazy right?

GOD is so good. I am so thankful that Junior stopped to talk to her. She's my heart and it's possible that neither one of us would still be here today, but we are.

In a Daze

Ace was furious about the robbery. He tried calling dude I suspected and when it became difficult to find him he knew it was true. He knew that MF set me up. Although I didn't want to talk to anyone, there was somebody I had to call. I called Big Dee. You see, before Ace had gotten locked up, somebody she knew sent some dudes to her apartment to rob her too. They ran up in her spot with the guns drawn for that paper. The fucked up thing was that they pushed her chick out the window. She didn't die, but she landed on her head and was never the same afterwards. And that was right next to the 30th Precinct. Those stick-up kids were bold. Some dudes got a lot of balls. But that's the risk they'll take for that money. They got away that day too.

Big Dee understood exactly what I was going through. "Anything done in the dark will come to light," she told me. That was the first time I heard that saying, but it wouldn't be the last.

Sometimes I didn't know if I was coming or going. You see, I wasn't going to be satisfied until something was done. I was raised around dudes that loved me and never wanted to see anything happen to me. That robbery shit had to be dealt with and I wasn't going to rest until it was handled. I was obsessed with getting revenge. I tell you something else too, I couldn't stand to look at that safe anymore. I rolled that shit into one of my mother's closets, threw a sheet over it, and never touched it again.

I was in a daze. That robbery had me fucked up, especially financially. It wasn't that I was broke, but I had to be smart about how I spent my money. Fortunately, my big pregnant belly allowed me to buy cheap shit and still look cute. I went shopping up on Broadway and bought some colorful jumpsuits. Guess how much I paid for them? Five fuckin' dollars. NO LIE. Like I said, it wasn't that I didn't have money, but there were more important things than clothes that it had to be used for.

I wasn't on my own though. Hen was there for me if I needed anything. And of course I reached out to Fat Boy because I knew he would be there for me.

"Who did it?" was the only thing he wanted to know.

Now, I just wanted to get the dude who orchestrated the robbery, but Fat Boy was like. "Everybody got to get it, the girl too. Since she wanted your ring so bad, we should cut her fucking fingers off when we catch her ass." Hearing that was like music to my ears.

That had been what I wanted to hear from Fritz, but he wasn't in the condition I needed him to be in. I knew Fat Boy wouldn't disappoint me. And I have to say that although Lou and I weren't together, he was still there for me pregnant and all. They loved me and when I hurt they hurt. Talking to Fat Boy made me feel much better. I wasn't sure if we would ever find dude, but I was satisfied to know that if we did justice would prevail. That street justice was real. Thinking back, I know it's not right to wish death on anyone, but at the time I was very angry and felt disrespected. I could've lost my baby. You know what I mean? Was it wrong of me to want them to suffer? Was it wrong of me to want to be judge and jury? Was it wrong for me to want to sentence them to death?

May was just not a good month for me, huh? Shit that year hadn't been good so far. What else could go wrong? I know some of ya'll dudes and chicks thought it was all about getting paper. Getting money was easy. The real risk was trying to keep it and stay alive. That life was not always what it seemed.

****

On June 13, 1991; Fritz called me and Henry down to 112th Street and gave us $40K to hire Mel Sachs to work with Levine on Ace's case. The next day, Henry and I jumped in his truck, I think it was a Forerunner, and raced downtown. That was around the time "Summertime" by Jazzy Jeff and the Fresh Prince came out. That shit was hot. It sounded crazy on Henry's booming system. Henry played that shit over and over. I think it was recorded over and over on the cassette tape he had. I remember that day clearly. The weather was nice, the windows were down, and we sped down the West Side Highway. Henry was my dude. In the midst of helping me out with Ace and making sure I was okay, he was still dealing with the fact that his brother and his girl caught a drug case because of him.

We walked into Sachs' office, looked at each other, and then we burst out laughing at the sight of Sach's. He was a peculiar looking dude who liked wearing bow ties. He was a famous lawyer known for crazy courtroom antics like using magic tricks to dispel the testimonies of witnesses. Quite a few celebrities had him on retainer. He showed me and Hen all the newspaper articles that had been written up on him. He was a showoff. We gave him the money, officially hiring him, and it was on. In my mind, we had Ace's case in the bag. We had the best lawyers and plenty of money, and all they had was a crack head witness. WTF!!!

"These motherfuckers need to throw the towel in now," I thought as Hen and I left Sachs' office.

The King is Gone
& The Queen Has Arrived

I got a call from Ace in July, and he sounded like he was in tears. I didn't know what was going on. At first I thought some dudes had tried to get at him on Rikers Island. Then he said he had called Fritz and someone had to hold the phone to Fritz' mouth but he could barely talk. That tore Ace to pieces. There was no way in hell those greedy MF's downtown could let Fritz get to that point. I said those dudes, but I'm really only talking about one. Someone told Ace that Fritz didn't want to go to the doctor. Ace said he screamed at them and told them to throw Fritz over their shoulders and take him to a fucking doctor. How could they sit there and let The King go out like that. Ace would've never let him wither away like that. He would've tried everything possible to keep him here. Fritz had family, but I'm not talking about them. Maybe ya'll might be thinking different. It's just my opinion.

Well, I'll tell ya'll right now. When someone has their eyes on the prize and greed has invaded their psyche, they can't see right from wrong. Yes, I'm sure Fritz knew it was almost over for him and he had to tell the next in line all the important info: Where all the coke was. Who all the customers and connects are. Where the money is. All that shit. All that MF saw was $$$$ signs. With Ace gone, nobody was there to take care of Fritz. He needed Ace. I know the feeling because I was having my baby without him.

My sister and Stan's wife, Yvette, decided to throw me a baby shower at my mother's house. It was July 13, 1991 and I was eight months pregnant. I didn't want to be bothered with anyone, but I ended up having a good time. I got so many nice things. Fat Boy and the 142nd street crew sent me some nice things. One of the biggest and most needed items was a stroller from Unique. I can't remember the name of the stroller, but it was an Eddie Bauer edition and it was $600. It came with a card that said "Even though it's not mine, Love Unique." Wow, I thought that was nice. I couldn't believe he did that, but then again I could because I dealt with real niggas. Dudes ain't built like that these days. These MF's today don't buy their own babies a stroller.

****

He's gone. KING FRITZ passed away on August 16, 1991. I know Ace was crying his eyes out. That was the most important and dear friend he had. That was his mentor. I was crushed. And it wasn't about the money I was getting because Fritz left instructions about that. I felt for Ace. Then I thought about The Family, La Familia. You know what I mean? Fritz' death left a deep hole in our lives and our hearts. He was going to be my baby's Godfather. I still consider him her Godfather.

****

I gave birth to Queen Tiana two days later on August 18. Unfortunately, I wasn't able to say farewell to Fritz. They took his body to South Carolina to bury him. The funeral was there too. Listen, this is when you know a real nigga has left us. They chartered buses to go down south to the funeral and anybody who wanted to go could ride those buses. The man was loved by so many people they had to make a way for people to be there for his funeral no matter what.

A few weeks after the funeral, I bumped into Fritz' wife down on 112th Street. She showed me some photos of him in the casket. OMG!!! He was handsome. The hair on his head and face was silky, jet black and curly. His skin looked smooth like velvet. It just broke my heart to see him like that and to know I would never see him again. There was a plaque in the casket. It was engraved with the image of two praying hands with the inscription "The World Was Mine And I Shared." Yo, I don't know who thought of that, but that shit was so dope because it was so true. I feel like crying right now because that summed up exactly the type of man he was.

Some prude right now might be saying, "Is she really

praising a drug dealer?" Excuse me, but yes the fuck I am. At that time that was my lifestyle. Yes he was a drug dealer, allegedly (LOL), but he was a great man who cared about people. He paid people's rent and no one on his block ever went hungry. His character is what I'm praising. The hood lost a good guy.

Ya'll know the saying, "Chop the head off and the body falls." Well, that's exactly what happened. Fritz was the head and once that head was gone so was La Familia. This MF I was speaking of earlier took over and just got real stupid. He cut all the family off and started messing with anybody and everybody else in Harlem, but the family. Hen, Big Dee and I were like WTF is he doing? That's the trifling shit I'm talking about. I know ya'll are waiting for me to drop that fools name, but I won't. He knows who he is. He and I had this talk a few times.

Check this shit out. He sent Al to come and tell me that he wasn't paying my bills no more. Oh hell nah!! Ace was hot when I told him that. That hit list of mine was getting longer. I was on fire. Yep, I went uptown to see Fat Boy because I wanted this dude gone too. It felt like it was open season on disrespecting ya girl.

Fat Boy and I sat down and talked. I told him what was going on.

"I hear you Tee," he said with a thoughtful nod. "But I can't do anything just yet."

Of course, I was waiting for an explanation like he worked for me or something. LOL.

"He's about to start hittin' us with some coke," he explained.

Yep. That's exactly what Fat Boy hit me with. "What! Hold the fuck up. Ya'll with me right?" Well, I didn't say it, but I damn sure thought it. He told me to chill because he was about to do some business with that greedy ass dude and that he would get the money from him for me. I didn't want the money anymore. It was the principle behind the matter. I'm glad I didn't have a gun, I probably would've shot Fat Boy in the ass too. LMAO
But fo' real though.

If that wasn't enough, Fat Boy's crazy ass goes, "Don't worry I got Tiana. That's my baby. I'll be her Godfather."

"Yeah, Yeah!" I thought as I stormed out of there mad as a motherfucker.

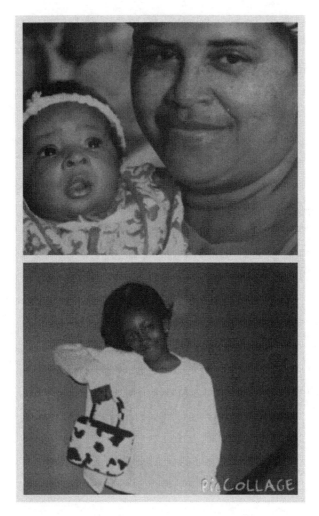

My Aunt and My Queen

Time to Make Moves

Fritz' passing was devastating in more ways than one. I decided to move out of both apartments. I could've kept the 2 bedroom, but I didn't like that terrace. It scared me, plus I wanted something new that nobody knew about. I wanted to start over. I found a huge 2 bedroom up on 162nd and Fort Washington Avenue. It was nice. When you first walked in there were two huge rooms that sat across from each other. I made one the living room and one the dining room. My bedroom was just as big as my living room and there was a nice size room for the baby.

One day I went to the apartment in 1199 to get a few things and there was something wrong with my locks. I called our personal locksmith Sloamy. He was a little short Russian guy. He let me in and changed the locks and I got a few things together and packed them up. I did all that by myself. I didn't want any help. I needed to be alone. I wasn't in the mood to really talk to anyone. Once I got there, I realized that being alone wasn't a good idea. I was losing everybody I loved and being near that terrace wasn't a good place to be. I left the apartment after a little while and decided to go to what did make me happy; my new baby girl.

****

In the meantime Hen started doing his thing in the Bronx. He had a lot to deal with. He went to see his brother and his girl every time they were allowed to get a visit. We all needed money because that dude that took over was on some other shit. It was just a crazy time for us. Dudes started acting funny about giving that money up. One day Hen called me and said, "Whoever didn't pay, I'm giving their names to the Colombians Fritz dealt with." I had no problem with that. I never met those Columbians, but it sounded like it could turn into a dangerous situation in the streets, but I didn't care. It was the principle. Ya know?

Big Dee called me one day and asked me to come uptown. When I got uptown to 143rd and 7th Avenue she introduced me to this fine ass dude named Jay Black. Big Dee had already told Jay Black who I was. This meeting was being set up so that we could get back on and begin to make moves to get us some money. Jay was real cool and very receptive to our needs. He was all in. He had what we needed. Big Dee was going to start off and when she got her thing going she would bring me in. This is what I mean when I talk about loyalty and looking out for each other. Jay Black could have been her best kept secret, but the love she had for me and Ace and the family period, would not allow her to be a sucka. It wasn't in her DNA.

It was fucked up that we had to be out there like that when what we needed was right downtown. But ya'll know karma is a motherfucker.

****

I was feeling kinda good and I needed to get back on my feet, so I went back to my apartment in 1199 to finish packing. This time, not only were my locks messed up again, but there was a paper on the door about some eviction bullshit. WTF!! Sloamy changed the locks for me again and then I went to the rental office to see what was going on.

Before I get to what happened let me explain how things went. Ace and Fritz were too busy to be paying rent and taking take care of small shit. So when you have guys like that, they delegate a lot of shit that needs to be done to other people. Of course they paid those people, trusting that things were getting done. They didn't have time to run behind people to make sure every little thing was done the way it was supposed to be. They assumed the people they paid did what they were supposed to do because there could be consequences if they didn't.

Back to this bullshit ya'll. I went to the rental office with the eviction notice and the office manager pulled the record. Get this shit. She said I owed $19,000 in rent. She said the rent hadn't been paid for three years. I damn near fell out. Who lets anybody live anywhere and pay nothing for three WHOLE years? The rent was mad cheap. Ace use to give this broad money to pay the rent so there was no way that lady was right. I even gave the chick that worked for Ace money to buy new blinds and all kinds of shit, just to keep the apartment looking nice. Not to mention I paid her to keep the apartment clean.

I went to St. Nick projects and dragged her ass back to that damn rental office. She sat there in front of the rental manager looking all crazy and crackish.

"I paid ya'll," she yelled out.

The lady looked her dead in her eyes and said, "No you didn't."

I looked at that broad like "Really Bitch." I knew the rental people weren't lying, but I had to ask, "How could ya'll let this go on for 3 years?"

I wished Ace and Fritz were around. They would've whipped her ass. I just took my furniture and put the furniture from both old apartments into my new apartment. Thank GOD I was leaving anyway. I called a company and had gates put on all my windows. Now when I say gates, I mean GATES. They cost me some change, but I wasn't gonna have a repeat of what happened in May. I had too much to protect like my life and my daughter's life. I couldn't wait for Ace to get out of jail. It was like I had to GTFO of 1991 and take my baby girl with me. You know what I'm saying? DAMN!

Ace had a lot of money tied up in the streets, but with having a new baby, having to pay the investigator, moving and just needing to have some extra money, Ace was worried and told me to go downtown to a bodega on St. Nicholas Ave to see one of his connects. That same connect had contacted me earlier in the year asking to buy the BMW, but I had told him no. This time I was going down there to offer it to him. I still had the Acura and the customized van. I also had Ace's Suzuki 1100. Everybody was asking to buy that bike. It was nice. Anyway, I charged the connect $9000 for the BMW and he gave me $4500 up front. I gave him the title and told him he could give me the rest of the money in a few weeks. I had no problem with him owing me the rest. He was the connect, right?

That $4500 paid the rent for a few months. I also had money saved up, but that was for any unexpected legal fees and feeding and clothing Ace. The crazy thing is that me and the baby never stayed at the new apartment. I let my oldest sister Janine and my nephew stay there. I still had my room at my mom's and that's where I was. I was 22 and a new mother. I needed help with my Queen. My aunt was there every day helping me and babysitting. I had to be in the streets. Every few days, I drove through different blocks trying to pick up a little money here and there. I had to make moves.

Say It Ain't So

Ace started trial early in 1992. I was excited and nervous at the same time. I just knew he was coming home. There was no way they could convict him on the testimony of a crack head. Oh yeah, she said she had watched the murder from a window while she was smoking crack. I mean she was literally smoking crack and watching the murder at the same time. You believe that shit? From what I knew, crack heads didn't multitask while they got high. Now it was another story when it came to them getting money to get high. When it came to getting money to get high they could multitask like a motherfucker. Ya'll know what I'm talking about. Those crack heads had unspeakable talents. They could change a lock, replace your transmission and run wires to get you free cable all in the same hour. WHAT! I'm not encouraging crack smoking, but crack heads came in handy. Seriously though, let me get back to where my head was at around the time the trial started.

With Fritz gone, and Ace starting trial, I was kind of stressed out. I didn't know what to do. Since that MF that took over 112th was on some bullshit, me and Hen decided we had to do our own thing. If I could count on anybody, I could count on Hen. One day Hen pulled up to my block in a brand new Acura NSX and hopped out wearing a purple suede jacket with fringes swinging from the sleeves.

"Look at my boy." GQ 24 hours a day," I thought to myself.

He was the funniest and flyest dude I knew. Me and Lil Sis couldn't get enough of watching him. He came through that day so we could put our heads together to figure out what to do. The first thing on his agenda was to get all the money left on the streets. Ya'll know I had already started getting some of Ace's paper. Hen was talking about money that was owed to Fritz. No matter what, we expected dudes to act like men and do business like men, but there was always somebody that had to act crazy. Money does that to people. But you know how that goes. Out of sight, out of mind and Fritz was gone and Ace was out of sight. Henry and that crab ass dude tried to collect some of Fritz' paper and this one nigga had the nerve to say "I can't pay a dead man," which meant he wasn't giving up any dough. GOD bless him. That dude didn't live too much longer after that statement, allegedly. At least that's what I heard.

Hmmmm.

It was about to get crazy out there. I guess dudes thought I was soft because I had a pussy, like I wasn't going to be persistent about getting that paper. WRONG! I was on those niggas' blocks every other day. Some dudes did the right thing and gave what they had, but there were some who claimed to be broke. In a way, I couldn't even blame them, but fuck that I needed mine. You see, dudes got nervous when Fritz died. They didn't know who was going to have the work (cocaine). A lot of dudes were trying to hold on to what they had. The streets were hurting. That MF that took over was shitting on people and only fucking with a select few. Hen and I should've passed that MF's name to the Columbians. I'm just saying. Like I said, Henry was the only one I could count on. He was the only one from downtown that kept it real. No matter what he was dealing with, he still found the time to call me every other day and when he had time he would stop by my block to see me. Just being able to talk to him gave me comfort. It was all love. He knew the meaning of family. That's how it's supposed to be when dudes go to jail or die in the streets. Real niggas take care of their partners' families. They don't leave anyone for dead. Unfortunately Fritz never knew homie wasn't a real nigga to begin with.

It seemed as though nothing else could go wrong, but everybody knows the saying, "When it rains it pours." That is so true. Little did I know I had a lot of stormy days ahead of me. Like I said before, and I say it today, I had a great upbringing, but my association with certain individuals got me into situations I never knew I would be in, let alone get out of. I got caught up in situations that a lot of men wouldn't have been strong enough to deal with, but I was. I thank GOD every day for getting me out of those situations.

****

"No GOD! NO!" My heart was crushed on May 13, 1992.

Henry was murdered in the Bronx. The one who cared about keeping the family together was gone. The 112th Street family that is. The only one who cared about me and Ace's daughter was gone. The only one who cared about making sure that whoever owed Fritz paid up was gone. He was buried six days later. The funeral was packed. He was loved by many, and I couldn't believe that seeing him in that casket would be the last time I would see him. His wife laid him to rest the same way he had lived, in style. It was more of a celebration, yet sad. He looked very dapper with a pair of sophisticated eyeglasses resting on his face. I was torn up inside at the funeral. I paid my respects, but I felt like that just wasn't enough to pay him back for all he had done for me.

R.I.P Hen Dog. You are still truly missed.

Twenty To Life

J udgment day came for Ace around June 1992. During his trial, we had been in court every day. Earlier I didn't bother to mention how at one point my friend Michelle and I were thrown out the court room for threatening a witness, but anyway I knew my man was coming home. We had the best lawyers and even the judge looked at the witness suspiciously from time to time, especially when she came in there looking crazy wearing bright red lipstick and gold fingernails. Ya'll remember those glue on gold nails? That bitch looked crazy. I just knew we had the case in the bag. Plus I knew one of the jurors. He was a dust head from my building, but he knew what to do. We expected a not guilty verdict or a hung jury. Either one would have worked. How lucky was that to have someone I grew up with on the jury?

"GUILTY," the jury foreman announced when the verdict came in.

I looked at that dust head motherfucker from my building like I could've put a bullet right between his eyes and killed him right there in the courtroom. Judge Renee White sentenced Ace to Twenty years to life. She said she spared him the extra five years she could've given him because she saw how much his family supported him. I could've slapped that bitch. She knew he wasn't guilty. She knew that case was bullshit. The Prosecutor, Assistant DA Sitnic, was a crooked bitch. That 25th Precinct had been out to get Ace. That precinct was full of shit. Half of those motherfuckers ended up going to jail or getting fired for corruption anyway. How were they credible? Ace was set up by somebody, and I was determined to find out by who. I think that was the worse day of my life. Fritz would've gone bananas if he was there.

I went home that day and cried. I never felt so lonely. I just looked out the window and sobbed. My world was crumbling around me. Everybody was leaving me. What was I going to do without Ace? How was I going to raise my daughter without her father? Ace hadn't even seen his daughter yet. I had refused to take her to Rikers Island for obvious reasons. I had witnessed other women who brought their babies to visit people there. The CO's went through the babies' diapers and mothers had to damn near get their babies naked. Nah, I wasn't putting my daughter through that. But with the way the trial turned out, I had to take her to see him. He needed to see his daughter. He hugged her so hard during the first visit. I saw the pain in his eyes. I felt so bad. What could I have done to make him feel any better? Marriage is what he wanted, but I just couldn't do it. I told him we should wait.

Within the next month, I paid $25,000 for the appeal and another $5000 to the private investigator, making it a total of $95,000 spent on that bullshit case up until that point. I used the money I had stashed in my apartment uptown. I was going to do whatever I could to get Ace out of there.

Tragedy Does Not Escape Me

I know ya'll are going to have a whole lot to say about me now, but I don't care. Listen, I was young. Do ya'll realize what I had gone through in the last year and a half? My man got locked up, I was tied up and robbed, my people were dying and my man got twenty years to life in prison. WTF!! I was handling a lot.

Okay so in the summer of 1992, I ran into this guy I grew up with. I actually use to be scared of him when we were kids. You know how when you're young there's always a crazy kid around that everybody's scared of. Well, he scared me. He had a big head and always looked mean. I can't say his name, but I'll just call him Paulie. He was bad when we were younger, but when I saw him that summer it was like love at first sight and we started messing around. I never would've thought I would mess with him. Maybe I was just looking for someone to love me. Who knows? I know it wasn't that long after Ace was convicted, but hey, my life had to go on. Twenty years to life sounded like one hundred years to me at that time. I couldn't see that far.

Paulie was down with one of the strongest crews in Harlem. His crew was led by a guy that was feared by many. Sorry guys, but I can't say his name either, but he was a good looking dark skinned dude from... Nah I can't say that either because then you'll know. LOL. Anyway, Paulie was quiet, but lethal. From what I've heard, he was the handyman of that crew. It didn't take long for me and Paulie to get tight. He had a girl, but you know how that goes. We started spending a lot of time together. We were together almost every day. We went out to eat, hit the movies, and just sat and talked about old stuff. He loved that song "Reminisce" by Mary J Blige. He popped that in the tape deck every time he got in my car. We listened to that song over and over and over.

Unfortunately, our relationship was short-lived. And when I say short, I mean short. I paged him one night to see what time we were getting together and he said he'd call me back later because he was out eating with a friend. He never called back.

I was driving uptown the next morning when this dude I knew called out to me when I stopped at a light on Bradhurst Avenue. I pulled over and this dude told me that they found Paulie dead in the Bronx. But that's not all he told me.

"I heard his people are looking for you," he said.

"Me? What the fuck they looking for me for?" You better believe a bitch was nervous. Like I said, the leader of that crew was the truth and I didn't want any parts of him.

"They said you were the last one he was with," he explained. "Oh hell no," I thought and sped off on that motherfucker. I didn't know what to do. I had to fix that shit. I wasn't into setting niggas up. All I could think about was those niggas coming after me for some bullshit. I went uptown and bumped into someone from Paulie's crew. I can't say his name either, but the news of Paulie's murder was no surprise to him. I told him about what that dude had told me and he calmly assured me I had nothing to worry about and said everything was fine. That's right, "Fine." What the fuck did he mean that everything was fine? Paulie was dead and nobody from his crew seemed to care. It seemed like some inside shit to me. That's when I knew I needed to leave well enough alone. "Damn, they got my baby." I don't know what he did to cause his own demise, but I guess he had to charge it to the game.

Back to that grimy ass nigga that lied about them looking for me. Ya'll wanna know why he said that? Well, he had liked me for years and I would not mess with his ass. I remember he tried talking to me one day when I was walking up to the Rucker game.

I resisted and he said, "I'm gonna get somebody to kidnap your ass."

It wasn't what he said, it was how he said it. You see, he was one of those dudes that could possibly make that happen. I told Stan because they knew each other. Anyway, back to why I think he told me that bullshit about people looking for me. So one day this clown saw Paulie driving my car with me in the passenger seat and I swear I saw the envy in his eyes as we rode passed him. I guess he assumed that 'Paulie" and I were a couple and got mad. But of course he wasn't going to approach Paulie about it. Telling me that bullshit was his way of getting back at me for not fucking with his ass. I couldn't believe that motherfucker had me running around thinking dudes were out to kill me. Niggas are real funny when you don't give them the pussy.

Seriously though ya'll, that shit with Paulie getting killed had me fucked up. My life was not what I wanted it to be. I dealt with more murders and heartaches than any young chick or human being should've had to deal with. That was it. I didn't know what to do. I know I needed to get a job or go back to school or something. I got focused on working and taking care of my daughter. Ace continued to work on his case, trying to prove his innocence, and I continued taking our daughter to visit him so they could get to know each other. She had a right to know who her father was. It wasn't his fault he wasn't around.

That day never came for Big Dee to get with Jay Black to get her money up. The FEDS snatched her up. When it rains it pours. I ended up selling my Acura Legend at the end of that year as well as the bike and the van. Times were getting hard and this year turned out to be worse than the last. But the devil wasn't done with me yet. Actually GOD wasn't done with me yet.

Mecca Audio

If you heard about Unique before you read this book, you already know about Mecca Audi and Club 2'G's. This MF threw the best parties. It was around '93 or '94. I can't really remember, but every Wednesday night Unique rented out this club called Club 2000. It was on 157th Street between Broadway and Amsterdam Avenue. I think the Dominicans had it on Fridays and Saturdays. My girls and I were there every Wednesday night. I never missed a night.

I don't care what anybody says. Club 2G's was the hottest shit happening on a motherfuckin' Wednesday night that year. I loved my Final Four parties, the Mirage etc., but Club 2G's was on another level. Ya feel me? The dance floor lit up with different colors with smoke coming out of it and the drinks stayed flowing. My girls and I got in free every week. At that time, I needed to have a good time because things weren't going well for me. Like I said before, being around Unique was like a party in itself so when he was given the chance to throw a party, it was on. Everybody who was somebody was in Club 2G's. Lil Sis says she remembers seeing Dre & Snoop, Redman and a few other rappers up in there. Sometimes Unique had male and female strippers there too. I'm telling you, he was considered a real nigga with no artificial preservatives. He was about his word, having fun, and just doing him.

He knew people from New York, to Cali, to Miami, and they all came through. That club was sick. I remember he brought Luke and some of Luke's dancers up from Miami. Niggas went bananas up in that spot. Ya'll remember Luke had some bad bitches back then? Unique had brought this male stripper from DC, I think, named Slick that claimed to be 12 inches long. You know the girls and I had front row seats for his show. After seeing that shit for real, I was like that's one dick he could keep. Bitches always running around talking about they want a big dick, but you couldn't pay me to fuck that dude. After the show, Unique introduced me and my girls to Luke's dancers and Slick. Unique was the man. Think about it. To pack a club in the middle of the week on a Wednesday night, and every Wednesday night at that, you know he had to be doing something right. That shit was jumping. Motherfuckers didn't care if they had to work, go to school or whatever; they weren't missing Club 2G's and neither was I. And you better believe I bought a new outfit every week for that club.

The main thing was that we had fun. We had a ball. Oh, and did I mention that it was only $5 to get in. That's right. You see, Unique wasn't throwing those parties to make money. He didn't need to make money from it; it was all about having a good time. Everybody had a good time drinking, laughing, and dancing with Harlem's own Tone Wop. Since Club 2G's, partying hasn't been the same. I wish we could get those days back.

I gotta tell ya'll the funny shit that happened to me. It was serious, but funny. Like I said before we went shopping every Wednesday for Club 2G's. I thought I was cute. I had on a tight fitted skirt suit and a long leather shearling that Ace left me. So one night before we went to the club, we all stopped at our girlfriend's house in the projects. We use to drink that 151 straight, no chaser. This night I didn't eat anything, but I was drinking that 151. All I remember is getting to the club and buying one of my sisters' friends a drink and that was it. I fell out.

I don't remember anything. The story is that I was so fucked up and my crew was so thirsty to party that they sat me in a corner with some shades on looking crazy. Then Lil Sis and one of her friends decided to put me in a cab, take me home and then go back to the club. Stan walks up and sees them struggling in front of my building, curses them out and sends their asses back to the club. Now anybody who knows Stan knows he's a funny motherfucker. All I know is that I woke up the next morning in the Bronx at his wife house with some small ass jeans on and some white leather skips that did not belong to me. I couldn't believe that shit. He had me looking real crazy, but that's what I get for slippin'. No matter what, Stan has always held me down and I love him for that.

Club 2G's was the talk of the town. Harlem was buzzin'.

Dudes that never went to clubs came out and made first appearances. You see, a lot of dudes that were getting money in Harlem weren't into too much clubbing. They made their money, flossed and balled out of control, and then went in the house or to the hotel with that special lady. But those Wednesday nights at Club 2G's gave way to curiosity. Those dudes that usually didn't go to clubs made an exception, just to see what was going on. There were never any fights or bullshit going on up in that club, which may have been the main reason they felt comfortable coming out. Well, that and their desire to know WHO THE HELL UNIQUE was and what was going on in that club everybody was talking about.

Unfortunately, a lot of those money-making dudes that came out back then are dead now. Even more unfortunate is that Unique ended up in federal prison, marking the end of the line for partying at Club 2G's. It was over, a wrap. Harlem never partied uptown like that again and never will. It's crazy though because for Unique the party is never over. I heard this dude incited a riot in Lewisburg Federal Prison. They said he was on the tables screaming, "Aaayyyoo Aaight!" Ain't that some shit. He called me when he got out the hole. "Yo Black, they beat me so bad my celly had to stitch me up." I just shook my head.

Of course there were and still are other parties in Harlem, but there could never be another Unique. No one could do what he did. I see some of ya'll out here throwing ya'll little parties. I don't care how packed ya'll parties are, the atmosphere is just different. He brought the hood together and made it fun. Thanks UE, you did your thing kid. Much love and hope to see you in the streets soon. We gotta do it again, Club 2G's 2015. LOL.

Me & lil Sis

Who Shot Ya?

I passed the time doing what I needed to do to survive. I hustled here and there, but it was like I lost it. I just didn't feel like doing it. Fat Boy was there for me and the baby. He called me one night and told me to bring the baby downstairs in fifteen minutes. I didn't know what he wanted. I thought maybe it was about daycare for Tiana. She was turning 3 soon. I wanted to put her in daycare, Tiny Tots Academy, and had asked him to pay for it. The cost was $320 a month and he said he'd pay it, so I thought maybe that's what he wanted. He came and we talked for a minute before he said, "Lou wants to know if that's his baby."

Now didn't I tell ya'll before that I was dodging sperm because I wanted to do me? LOL… Yes, I did get pregnant before, but I had a miscarriage. I wasn't one of those trifling chicks that be trying to get pregnant by dudes or caught up in a bunch of "Who's the father?" nonsense. I looked Fat Boy in the eye and told him, "She is not Lou's daughter. Ace is her daddy." I could understand why Lou may have wanted to know. It wasn't that long after us that I got pregnant by Ace. Still though, I thought it was cute that he wanted to be her daddy. But Ms. Tee don't play those games. Nope.

At that time, I had already given up the other apartment and was living with my mom. I had so much furniture that I was able to furnish my mother's entire apartment, give some to my aunt and sell some to a friend named Sean that hustled out in DC. I also gave a bar full of liquor to two of my mother's neighbors. I lost everything and almost everybody, but I still had my family though. They held me down.

****

Remember I told ya'll GOD wasn't done with me yet. Well, my life took another turn on July 14, 1994. Me and Shelli's lil sister were walking up my block after coming from the Jamaican Hot Pot restaurant on 7th Ave when I saw some dudes from Lou's crew talking to a friend of mine named Fifty. I knew Fifty all my life. We were in kindergarten together so we went way back.

Let me explain to ya'll who Fifty was to my block. You know how your block has one or two thorough dudes that hold shit down? HOLD SHIT DOWN. I had to say that twice. I'm talking about dudes that never let anyone come to the block and act crazy. And if somebody did, it was LIGHTS OUT. Yeah, that was Fifty to my block. There was another dude too, but he was away at the time. Nobody from the block had heart like they did. Remember what I said earlier about Fritz dying and how there should've been every attempt to make sure he was okay before he died? Ya'll remember that? That's because when you have someone that is The King or That Nigga that will kill for you and make sure the block is protected no matter what, his boys are supposed to always be there for him. I'll say it again, "When the head falls the body will rock."

Anyway, I knew something was up on the block that day, so instead of going upstairs I attempted to wave a cab down to run uptown to see Fat Boy. I raised my hand and all I heard was, POP! POP! POP! I turned and saw Fifty running towards me from down the block with a look on his face I will never forget. There was a huge red circle on his chest. Now, there are different stories about how he ended up on the block talking to them in the first place, but I'm not going to say anything about that. Ya'll have to understand something. Fifty NEVER went anywhere without his gun and he had a look of disappointment on his face as he ran towards me. It was like "DAMN, how I let these MF's catch me out here like this?"

I turned and ran from him as he ran towards me, and the shooters were on both our asses. I made it across the street and tripped on the curb or something. I looked up and saw Shelli's lil sister standing there in shock with her hands covering her face. Fifty ran pass me and fell to the ground a few feet away. I don't remember feeling anything, but I yelled out "I'm hit."

All at once a scene of me and Fifty lying under white sheets ran through my mind, a scene I had already seen so many times in my life. Then I thought about Ace and who was going to take care of the baby. I couldn't leave my baby girl so I got up and jumped in a cab like a trooper. I got to Harlem Hospital and they immediately rushed me in, tore my clothes off and began working on me.

A 9mm bullet went through my back and tore through my chest, hitting my lung on the way out. They rolled Fifty in while I was on the emergency room table. I watched them split his chest open and massage his heart in an attempt to revive him.

"Come on Fifty, Come on." I silently encouraged looking over at him. I wanted him to make it. I needed him to make it. The block needed him to make it. He died right next to me.

I fell unconscious and the next thing I heard was a thick Jamaican accent saying "Dats mi dawta," Yeah, Keith was in the building. He came up to me while I was laying there and said, "Ms. Tee. Ooo didit?" Ooo shot ya?"

I think I told ya'll before that my daddy was wild and had no problems laying somebody down. I was like, "Daddy, don't worry. I got this." Wasn't that some shit. I was lying up there talking about I got something. SMH. He put his index finger to his lips, signaling me not to tell the police anything, which meant he wanted to handle it in the streets. LMAO. Allegedly, he killed someone many years earlier for disrespecting his grandmother. That's what I heard. I know for a fact he crippled a man and had to flee Jamaican in 1991 and couldn't go back for 15 years, leaving all his money behind.

They said Keith was outside asking if anyone knew anything. My daddy loved his kids. My Lil man Roc (Maine's friend) was outside crying and damn near broke the glass outside Harlem Hospital, I heard. They say the crowd out there was crazy. The news stations had set up on Lenox Avenue. One reporter crept up on my sister and Shelli.

"Oh, I'm so sorry for you. What happened?" the reporter said.

Before they could respond, the reporter whistled and the next thing they knew she had a microphone in her hand and there was a camera and bright lights pointed at their faces. Their ashy faces that is, because they had been crying for ya girl. Those reporter MF's always gotta get a story.

After that my sister, her boyfriend, Shelli and Roc went up to 142nd Street. Now my lil sister has that official crazy Jamaican shit in her, and she went uptown to let some of that crazy shit loose. And that's exactly what she did. This is how she told me it went down.

She went to the bodega on the corner of Lenox Avenue and somebody said, "You can't go in there. They're having a meeting."

"Fuck that. They shot my sister," she yelled, prompting Fat Boy, Lou and some of the shooters to walk out the store.

"All ya'll motherfuckers are going down." Ya'll shot Tee," she yelled before pointing at the shooters saying, "Yeah, it was you, you and you." Now mind you, we were cool with everybody that was down with Lou's crew. My sister knew which ones had done the shooting by the descriptions the witnesses gave.

Lou was speechless as she spoke. He had no idea I had been shot. She said the look on his face was of pure shock. She said he looked like he wanted to cry. Shelli said Lou just put his head down. Fat Boy hugged Lil Sis and promised, "Don't worry. She's going to be okay. I got somebody over there."

Later that night, I sat in my hospital room watching the news report on what had happened. I watched it all night. They had red flares in the street where it happened along with those numbered cards that indicate how many shell casings were on the ground. According to the news report, four guys and one girl were shot with one pronounced dead. The news cut from the crime scene and I saw Michelle on the news. It was some real movie type shit. Although it was Lou's people that shot me, by mistake, I think, I was still scared. I didn't think they would hurt me, but I still requested that my name not be put in the system and that security should guard me.

Some fucking security. Guess who came walking in the room, pushing a medical cart with a white doctor's jacket on? Fat Boy. Now what if he didn't have love for me or felt he couldn't trust me? I would've been dead. Have ya'll been paying attention? Why the fuck wasn't security ever looking out for me? They let me get punched in the eye by Cal, punched in the face by Lou, tied up and robbed in my house and damn near smothered in my hospital bed. LMAO! But for real, my luck with security hadn't been good so far. Fat Boy kept apologizing for what happened. Like I said, I already thought it was a mistake.

I was in the hospital for seven days. There was a little box that looked like a suitcase on the side of my bed. There was a tube connected to it that went into my chest to drain the blood out of my lungs while I received 3 blood transfusions.

Earlier I said the devil wasn't done with me, but then I said GOD wasn't done with me. This is what I was talking about. Although I know it was all GOD, I'm stronger than a motherfucker ya'll. Anybody else would've laid there on that curb shot the fuck up and waited for an ambulance. I know a lot of men that laid there and waited for an ambulance and didn't make it. Ya girl wasn't going out like that. I'm glad I didn't lay there and wait. Something made me get up. Had I not gotten up, blood would've filled up my lungs and smothered me to death.

Remember I also told ya'll earlier that I was on Lou and his co-defendants' indictment? This is why. Him and his crew were on there for Fifty's murder and attempt on the lives of me and those three other dudes that got hit.

After Fifty was killed, I felt some type of way. I didn't like the way that shit went down. I'm sure Fifty was involved in something, but I felt like me and my girls needed to do something for him. Fifty wasn't a saint by any means, but I don't get down with snake shit. When people decide to set a MF up, they don't realize who else can get caught up in that bullshit. I could say more, but I'm not going to.

I was determined to do something special for the first anniversary of Fifty's death. I knew this dope artist named Es from uptown, so on July 15, 1995; I gave him Fifty's picture and some money and he did what he does best. The painting looked just like Fifty. Es put me and my girls' name on the painting. We threw a party outside for Fifty. If I'm not mistaken Fifty took his name after some legendary dude from Brooklyn named Fifty Cent. I think he's gone now too.

Getting shot fucked me up for a minute. I had to see a psychiatrist because I couldn't sleep. Actually I refused to go to sleep. That's what it was. I was so tired, but whenever I started to fall asleep I fought it. The only way I can explain it is to say that every time I was falling asleep I felt like death was coming to get me, so I refused to go to sleep. It was weird. The doctor put me on Valium to help me sleep. Yo! That Valium is the truth. Oh yeah, when I was in the hospital they gave me Demerol for pain. That shit was the truth too. That shit took all the pain away. They shot me in my arm so much with that shit that my skin got tight and the needle wouldn't go in.

It's twenty one years later and I still have problems from that shooting. I developed Post Traumatic Stress Disorder (PTSD). Whenever I hear POPPING sounds or if a book or something flat hits the floor, I jump so hard that sometimes it's embarrassing. Certain sounds that wouldn't normally scare someone like you scare the shit out of me, but I deal with it. Shit, I have no choice but to deal with it. I could probably get a check for this shit. Get me some SSD with my crazy ass.

That's my boy Fifty right there. That's a real dude ya'll looking at. No bullshit.

FIFTY

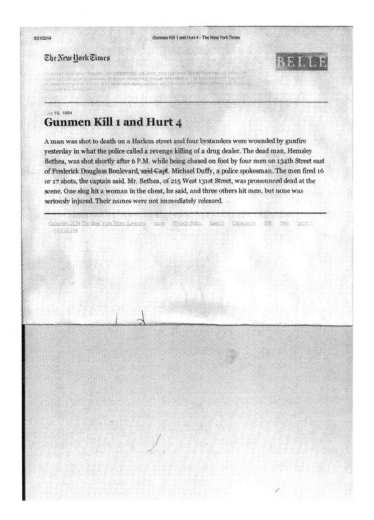

5/31/2014   Gunmen Kill 1 and Hurt 4 - The New York Times

The New York Times

BELLE

...ly 15, 1994

Gunmen Kill 1 and Hurt 4

A man was shot to death on a Harlem street and four bystanders were wounded by gunfire yesterday in what the police called a revenge killing of a drug dealer. The dead man, Hemsley Bethea, was shot shortly after 6 P.M. while being chased on foot by four men on 134th Street east of Frederick Douglass Boulevard, said Capt. Michael Duffy, a police spokesman. The men fired 16 or 17 shots, the captain said. Mr. Bethea, of 215 West 131st Street, was pronounced dead at the scene. One slug hit a woman in the chest, he said, and three others hit men, but none was seriously injured. Their names were not immediately released.

The Lynch Mob Gets Hung

Lou was arrested on August 29, 1994; about a month after I got shot. He was accused of participating in a shooting that happened on the afternoon of the day he got arrested. Over the next year, Lou and his whole crew were all over the news. Lou and his people had no idea that they had been under federal investigation for the previous year and a half. They were arrested one by one and charged and indicted on Murder, Attempted Murder, Drugs, Racketeering, Conspiracy, and of course the shooting that involved me and Fifty. I knew they weren't getting out of that. The reign of the 142nd Street Lynch Mob came so a screeching halt. It was over. They made the front of the paper, so you know it was big. One of the headlines read, "10 Gang Members in Harlem are indicted." The article by Ronald Sullivan read as follows,

For more than five years, the drug gang conducted what prosecutors called a reign of terror in central Harlem, murdering rival gangsters, shooting bystanders and terrorizing the neighborhood surrounding Lenox Avenue and 142nd Street. Gang members even entered Harlem Hospital Center in hospital whites last year, prosecutors said, in an unsuccessful effort to stab a rival drug dealer whom they had failed to kill a few days earlier despite shooting him 15 times.

Didn't I just tell ya'll that MF came up to my room with a white jacket on? Ya'll thought I was lying. Those MF's were official with that killing shit...... Allegedly. I can't forget that. LMAO.

They were arresting members of that crew up until June of 1995. Of course, Lou's name was at the top of the indictment. Seeing their photos and the headlines in the newspapers was just overwhelming and real. The streets were really buzzing. Like I said before, they claimed the murder rate went down 56% with Lou and his crew off the streets. I know some of ya'll might know who Lou is. I know some of y'all might not like him. I'm not saying that anything he did was right. I'm just saying that the hood took what was being said about him and ran with it. People were blaming him for things he didn't do. We all know who killed Rich Porter, yet I received a threatening phone call about his murder. Lou is fully aware that the crimes he committed were wrong.

Well after the arrest, most of the members of the Lynch Mob were held at M.C.C or Otisville Federal Prison up in Pennsylvania. Lou contacted me from Otisville. I believe Fat Boy and two other members were at M.C.C I didn't really care too much about the rest of them, so I don't know where they were. I maintained communication with Lou through phone calls and mail. Lou sent messages to Fat Boy through me and others that visited him at Otisville. I maintained communication between them by third party mail. He wanted to make sure him, Fat Boy and the others worked their case together. The FEDS eventually sent me letters stating that it was against the law to send third party mail, but I still found ways to get messages back and forth for Lou. The third letter stated that I could be prosecuted for sending messages, and I decided to fall back. I didn't want to risk getting locked up or becoming an accessory or conspirator to their shit.

Ya'll gotta watch the FEDS though. They're always looking for the weakest link. But one thing about the FEDS is that if they pick you up, it means they got your ass. Even if they have to make up lies to keep you, you're going down.

Lou went national with his shit. According to the FEDS he committed a murder in Louisiana and was sentenced to the Electric Chair for it. DAMN! I've never known anyone on death row. I'm not saying anything that's not in the papers, and in case you're wondering if Lou knows that I'm writing about him. Hell Yeah! That MF ain't coming after me. LOL. I'm just playing, but yes, he knows. He actually wanted me to expose a few RATS from his case, but I don't have time for no bullshit ass lawsuits. Ya know! Most people from Harlem know who they are and the snitches know who they are. That's just something they have to live with.

At the time he was caught up in those legal battles, all I kept saying was "I can't believe this." I mean, was this the man I knew, loved, cared about and made love to? I almost had kids with this man. Could he be the monster that everyone described? Why was I so quick to doubt what everyone was saying? I loved him so much and at that moment I realized that I still loved him, maybe even more. Was something wrong with me? 'Cause that's just crazy. I'm talking about me right now. But at the time he needed me and I was going to be there for him no matter what.

There was one guy still on the streets from the Lynch mob. I won't mention his name either. He was one of the more respected members because he was older. He called me one day and asked me to come downstairs so we could talk. The news was that a few members of the team started turning. He couldn't believe that some of the crew had turned so quickly. We agreed that everybody needed to get their asses up to Otisville to see Lou, and I told him I would take care of that.

Fat Boy was still in M.C.C at the time, and Lou was getting upset that it was taking him so long to get transferred to Otisville. Fat Boy claimed it was easier for his family to visit. I was like "fuck a visit you're trying to go home." I later found out he had other plans. Up until then I had been able to visit Lou at Otisville, but the visits stopped when the authorities threw him in the hole. He knew he didn't do anything wrong and tried to find out what the confinement was all about. They let him make a few phone calls and he called his lawyer and then called me. I'll never forget that phone call.

"Hey Boola," I said and then listened as he told me what was going on. "What? Testifying? That motherfucker," I yelled into the phone.

Shit was about to get crazy complicated. Where the fuck was the loyalty to the one who demanded that the streets respect you? Where was the loyalty to the one who made your problems go away? I didn't believe my ears. It started with one dude willing to testify, and then there was another and another and then another. I was like, "Damn." By the time it was over they had more than enough dudes that were willing to testify. Oh excuse me, not testify, I meant snitch like bitches, as Lou would say. The main nigga that everyone thought would fold, held his head and took ten years like a champ. He was the one everybody called a punk or a pussy, but he stood his ground and snatched ten years and skated. A good friend of mine got three years and got out. His involvement wasn't as serious as the others.

Oh, and homie that called me downstairs all upset because dudes were snitching, yeah him, he jumped on that train too. SMH!!!!

It was open season on Lou Sims. He had so many co-defendants snitching on him that they had to put him in the hole to make sure he didn't bump into anybody. Some were up in Otisville with him. The authorities knew that if he ran into any of them it wouldn't be a good thing. They ended up sending him to M.C.C. He told me he spotted Fat Boy mopping floors one day while he was on his way to a visit. I never visited Fat Boy, but we spoke on the phone and wrote letters to each other. That is, until one day he asked me about my shooting incident out of the blue. It didn't have anything to do with our conversation. I'm no fool. That was the last conversation I had with him.

I once asked Lou, "How do you feel about what Fat Boy is doing?"

I was surprised by his response. He said he still had love for him. Was he mad? Yes, but he knew snitching to get back at them wasn't the thing to do. Like he told me before, "Tee, I just wasn't raised like that.

That's when it hit me that he was one of the realest niggas I knew, probably one of the last. There are things that you have to think about in those situations, knowing that you might be back on the streets one day. How can you look people in the face knowing that you're a RAT? What ya'll think? I'm just saying. As for me, RESPECT is everything. No matter what the relationship is. Whether it's, lovers, friends, family, marriage... RESPECT and LOYALTY is EVERYTHING. Your word is your BOND. I have to be honest. I still have letters from Fat Boy and although what he did hurt me too, I still love him. He was a really good dude. Sometimes none of us know what we'll do in a situation. My only question for Fat Boy is, "WHY?"

I want to take this time out to give a shout out to Dame and Danny who from day one has always been there for Lou. I will never leave out my friend and brother Beatty. Lou definitely appreciates you guys.

Lou sent me a copy of the indictment, which included 15 murders and 5 attempted murders. He wasn't responsible for all those murders. He was guilty because he was Lou. I couldn't believe what I was reading. As I read the victims' names, I was like, "Damn, they killed him too. And that motherfucker too. I use to talk to that dude." When Lou reads this book I'm sure he's going to ask who I'm talking about. OH BOY!

Lou and I are not together, but is the love still there? Of course it is. Who don't still love me? LMAO. One thing I can say is that Lou supports me no matter what. Whether I'm with someone, married or whatever, his only question is: "Is he good to you?" Besides knowing him almost all my life, my happiness and well-being means everything to him, and now maybe ya'll can understand why he and I are so cool. Most dudes that had a relationship with a chick can't deal with seeing her with anyone else, and that's understandable. But a strong dude that respects you can and will support you no matter how they feel. I just had to explain that, but back to the story. Speaking of one of the murder victims on the indictment, I remember the night it happened. It was in the summer and I was pregnant at the time too. The dude had just drove by my building in a doom buggie. My sister was uptown with Unique. She came downtown in a cab and told us that dude had just been killed. We all jumped in my car and raced uptown. We got up there and saw him lying in the buggie with the music still blasting on 8th Ave. He never saw it coming. He had no idea that his life was about to end. Damn!! That was in 1991.

Lou ended up taking a plea and copped out to all known and unknown incidents/murders, which meant that if they found out about any other murders or crimes after the copout, he couldn't be charged. That means, if they find ten bodies buried right now and can prove that he did it back then, he can't be charged. That was a sweet deal. He took thirty years like a champ for his involvement in murders, drugs, conspiracy and racketeering. He snatched that up quick, like he hit the lotto. He did hit the jackpot though. MF's are in the system right now doing twenty-five for 1 murder and he only gets five more years for about fifteen plus bodies. And he don't have to do the whole thirty. That's the system for ya.

I know what ya'll thinking right now. Now if he had all these people that wanted to testify, why did they give him an offer? I'll tell you why. People started changing their stories and in order not to lose the case they gave him a deal. Those that turned got scared because they knew it wouldn't have been a good look if they actually had to take the stand.

The FEDS weren't finished with his ass yet though. He later found out that the copout didn't include the murder charge he had in Louisiana. He blew trial in Louisiana and was sentenced to death by electric chair. He later got that overturned. When it was all said and done, he ended up getting less time than some who told. Now I know ya'll wanna know how the fuck that happened, right? Well, when they started changing their stories their plea deals got torn up and they ended up with more time than Lou. Fat Boy didn't pull one trigger and Lou will be home way before him and another one of them. It's twenty one years later and Lou is short. I've been telling this guy how things have changed and hopefully he has too. We have these talks a lot about doing better and living for the kids and grandkids. But sometimes telling Lou to be good is like telling a baby not to shit in their diaper. LOL.

Snitching

For some years now snitching seems to have become a trend. I'm not talking about reporting a crime. There's a difference. A detective friend of mine told me something that made sense. He said there's a difference between a snitch and a witness to a crime.

"If you witness a crime upon someone that didn't do anything to anyone, you should report it because it could've easily have been you, your kids, your friends or a loved one," he reasoned. "A snitch on the other hand is someone who's telling to satisfy his own need. He's not telling to help someone out or to protect someone. He's being a selfish coward."

I'm not against telling on a rapist, molesters, or if someone is threatening your life or the lives of your family members, but I am against someone trying to ruin somebody else's life to regain their own freedom when they've committed just as many crimes as the next man. It's unacceptable and shouldn't be tolerated. Back in the day people's families were killed because of these acts of selfishness. I blame the FEDS in general for starting this trend of snitching.

The FEDS themselves can be some lying, cheating ass motherfuckers. They've manipulated dudes into a position to feel like snitching is the only way out, but it's still dudes fault for falling for that shit. Sometimes you have to just stand your ground and tell "The Man" to kiss your ass. If dudes would just shut the fuck up sometimes, half of them wouldn't be locked up now. Half the time, cops don't know shit until dudes open their mouths. I realized this many years ago. I can't understand how dudes haven't figured that out yet. I'm just saying, do your time and keep it moving. It's only fair. Let the police do their jobs. Although it helps the police really have no respect for snitches. A detective told me that too.

A lot of snitches come to mind as I write this, too many to mention though. Hey it is what it is. Or is it? FOH!!!!

It Ain't Trickin' If You Got It

T.I. said, "It ain't trickin' if you got it." Bullshit! Who the fuck made that up? Tell T.I. TRICKIN' is TRICKIN'. That's just an excuse dudes use so that they can spend money on chicks. Ain't nothing change. I'm from the old school and trickin' then and trickin' now is the same thing. And guess what? If you didn't have it you couldn't trick anyway. It's just that now the money is not the same as before, so trickin' has changed. Ain't no trickin' going on. To be honest with you, bitches are out here making their own money. Women are becoming more business minded. More of us are entrepreneurs now.

Speaking of trickin'. I started talking to this guy from Harlem around 1996. Everybody from Harlem knows him and dealt with him in some type of capacity. I honestly didn't start out wanting him at all. He sold drugs of course, and his money was long. It was long enough to start a bogus company and need the use of an accountant. He owned homes and boats and shit like that. He had a club too. I use to always see him at parties and different places. Like I said, it wasn't him that I wanted. I wanted one of his friends that worked for him. I wanted the worker bad. Don't judge me ya'll. Let me do what I do. The dude that worked for him didn't have money like that, but he was a bad boy and I liked that, obviously. He was rough. He was a quiet dude, but very dangerous. He never really went to parties so I was surprised to see him this one night.

One night we all, meaning Harlem, went to a party at the Mirage and he was there. The Mirage was the spot. We had a ball in there. There were those nights when Puff said wear Versace and everybody went out and bought Versace shirts, pants, shades and all. That's how we did it. The parties at the Mirage never disappointed. Of course Brooklyn had their asses in their too, but for the most part we always had a good time. A lot of rappers came through too. The name changed a few times too. It went from the Mirage to Exit and it was something else, but I can't remember. Oh yeah, the Carbon. I think that was it.

This particular night I had on a see-through dress. And you could see right THROUGH it. It was blue, green and yellow. Anyway, the worker dude and I were giving each other the eyes and shit, and I guess the dude with the money noticed it and started feeling some type of way. I didn't even know the dude with the money liked me, but ya'll have to understand something about how things go. Some people in the streets knew I was with Ace and that he had all this money. The streets talk. People will know all about your business and you've never even met them. That's just how the streets are. Before I go on let me explain to ya'll how shit goes in the streets. Niggas kill me. Maybe some will agree, but here it goes.

A chick ends up in a relationship with a dude that has a lot of money. All the other street dudes know him or heard of him, admire him and want to be like him. Then something happens that causes this chick not to be with him anymore. Maybe he got killed, went to prison or they just broke up. THEY ALL WANT HER NOW just because he (meaning the dude that had the money) had her. Niggas are crazy. They all want the bitch That Nigga had just because she was with him. Ya'll following me? Now I don't know why it's like that, but it is.

Back to me and this dude that had the money. So this dude slid right in and started talking to me. It was kinda rude and I know lil homie would've done him dirty, but sometimes dudes feel that since the other dude got the money the chick will choose him instead of them. No, because like I said I was on lil homie hard. But dude with the money came at me so hard, the MF got me. Yeah, yeah, I started messing with that MF. So what! He came at me saying how he had been wanting me, but he knew he didn't have as much money as ACE, blah, blah, blah. See, what I told ya'll? Niggas kill me. LOL.

His bogus businesses were just a front to hide his street money. One day he called me and told me that his accountant said he wasn't spending enough money and asked me if I wanted to go shopping. WTF did he think? HELL YEAH I wanted to go shopping. I didn't respond like that though.

"Oohkay," I innocently replied in a soft voice. My ladies know how we use that sweet voice when we want something.

He flew me out to Vegas to the Tyson and Holyfield fights, the Mayweather fights, and took other trips. We went to nice restaurants. He would just call me up and say come downstairs. He would hand me a bag with lingerie, or a coat or shoes. He was a good guy. He spoiled me and I loved it. I dealt with him off and on for like fourteen years. When I ended up in a relationship he was heated. It's not like he wasn't with anyone, so I couldn't understand why he was so mad.

He would ring my phone off the hook. You know how you call someone and if they don't answer you wait for them to call you back. Nah, not him. I would get fifteen calls straight back to back. He was on me hard. The Power of the Pussy is a crazy thing. LOL. He still gettin' money today. I know ya'll want to know who he is, but I don't always kiss and tell. At the end of the day, he's a good dude and a good friend. Plus I don't want certain people trying to lean on him because they mad he was messing with me. Ya'll know how that goes. See those were the type of dudes that were around back then. I remember those days well. To be tricked on was a beautiful thing. Honestly, I don't call it trickin' because when a woman knows her worth she's supposed to expect nice things. I dealt with some real good dudes as far as that paper is concerned, but money wasn't always everything. If I liked you, that was it. I like what I like and it doesn't always have to be about the money.

I have to say this about trickin'. Most of these Tricks had girls or wives or whatever anyway. That's why it was trickin'. Men ain't shit sometimes. That's the bottom line. They lied to their main girl or wife about going out of town to do business and took the ladies they were trickin' on away on trips. Sometimes us ladies would get more time, respect and money than wifey did. So, you figure it out. What you call that? I'm not saying it was right, I'm just saying.

When a woman's game is tight she can get a man to do anything. I know. Having the bomb pussy helps tremendously. When I was like 17, 18 or 19; I was telling dudes that I had to pay my mother's rent and shit like that. For the record my mom has never asked her kids to pay rent, and even though some of them fools never stepped foot in my house, they paid the rent. Oh excuse me, they thought they were paying the rent. LMAO! That was the Power of the you know what.

Again, trickin' is trickin'. I don't care if they got a little or a lot. If they're giving up that paper just to spend that time with you it's trickin'.

Me and Lil Sis

Me & Billy Sims, one of the best that did it
(Lou's older brother)-
Yacht party

Guess Who Stuck Me For My Paper?

Remember I got robbed and tied up back in 1991, right? Okay good. And ya'll remember what Big Dee said to me about anything in the dark will come to light? Guess what? Big Dee was so right about that. That's why if you're going to do something, you either do the shit alone or don't fucking do it at all. How about that? So anyway, it was the summer of 1996 or 1997. I was coming out of my apartment building when this lady that happened to be standing in the lobby flagged me down. She and her family lived in the building with us for years, so I knew who she was.

"You're Tonia, right?" she asked.

"Yes," I replied.

"I've been looking for you. I have something to tell you."

I was stunned and shocked because I had no idea what it was she could possibly want to tell me. It turned out that she was about to pull my coat about what went down when I got robbed 6 years earlier. The story was that this bitch I grew up with that lived in my building told the lady about the whole set up. This chick was best friends with the lady's daughter. Now me and this chick never hung out or anything like that, but she knew me well enough not to put my life in danger the way she did. According to the lady, Ace's cousin who happened to be the dude I suspected all along, had a baby by some chick whose brother went with the chick from my building. Are ya'll following me? Supposedly they all sat around a table and planned the robbery. The lady even told me what guns they had, which is how I was able to tell you about the guns earlier.

So when Ace's so-called cousin came to my house that night and left, the plan was in play and the robbery was a go. That's what money will do to greedy motherfuckers. I couldn't believe that bitch went along with that whole plan. It wasn't just greed, it was crack too. She had been on and off crack for a while, but I'm not excusing her. Like I said, I knew Ace's cousin had something to do with it all along. I just didn't know who all the players were and I wasn't interested in them either. Never worry about the puppets. It's the puppeteer you want when shit goes down like that. Always go after the one who orchestrated the show, but that in no way excuses her.

I eventually approached that bitch about what I found out and she tried to act like it was all Ace's cousin idea and that she had nothing to do with it, but even if it was, it was her man that helped mastermind the whole shit. She was lucky Lou and Fat Boy were already gone, because I would've had them cut her motherfucking fingers off. She is lucky I didn't mention her name too. Bitch.

Twelve years after the robbery is when I finally saw the cousin again. I had heard he started smoking crack too. I guess they all were a bunch of closet crack head motherfuckers.

You see that's how the game is played. Ain't nothing fair about The Game. You still got MF's out here plotting and shit, but ain't no money out here like that anymore. They're plotting on pennies. But then again, a little to somebody is a lot to somebody else who has nothing. That's why all that frontin' like you have what you don't have ain't worth it. You better believe that somebody's willing to try to take what they think you have, even if you really don't have it. Unfortunately, there are some specific frontin' ass dudes out in Harlem that are still trying to catch up to something that don't exist anymore. Especially for those of ya'll that have sons and daughters, get ya life right. If you think anybody cares about any of that shit, guess what?

WE DON'T.

DONALD: R.I.P

I would be remiss if I didn't mention Donald. He was the love of my life, but sadly, I'm not sure if he ever believed it. We were engaged and he knew I loved him dearly, but I always got the feeling he didn't think he was good enough for me. Why? I don't know. He was a drug dealer, but never a gangster. He made his money and was very low key. Although Donald was a little older than him, he was good friends with Mendeecees and his older brother. Ya'll know that dude from Harlem that's on Love & Hip Hop, I mean Lies & Hip Hop. Yeah, I got a story about a meeting I had with them MF's too at VH1. LOL. I'll tell ya'll about it another time.

Anyway, Donald was the sweetest person ever. He was caring, loving and very generous. He was more than eager to do whatever made me happy. I've basically lived my entire life without any regrets, except one. And I've said this over and over again, "I regret ending our relationship." I'll tell you why in a minute.

He was one of the most giving guys I ever met or dealt with. While we were together he bought me a truck, jewelry and furs, but the gifts didn't stop when our relationship ended. I remember I bumped into him one day a while after we broke up. I complimented him on this nice diamond cross he had on.

"Do you want one?" he asked.

"Yeah," I jokingly responded.

Do ya'll know that dude called me the next day so we could meet up? This man handed me a heavy chain with a beautiful diamond cross that he bought from Dibur on Route 4. That just speaks of who he was.

Okay, so let me tell ya'll this. I'm very big on health and going to the doctor. I use to always tell him to make sure that he gets regular checkups. Years after we broke up while I was living in Atlanta, I learned that he ended up in prison, had gotten very sick and was diagnosed with brain cancer. Now let me say that between our breaking up and his going to prison, he dealt with his share of chicks. Unfortunately, I feel that many of those chicks were more concerned about his money, and not his well-being. And that's where my regret comes in. I'm not saying I could've saved him, but he would've found out about his cancer far in advance. I would've made sure he got the best care necessary.

This brings me to a very important point. Black men, you must go to the doctor for regular checkups. For the life of me, I can't understand why you're so scared to go. The fact that a lot of you don't have medical or life insurance is a huge problem. You need to figure out how to address that problem, and quickly.

I came back to NY from Atlanta in June 2009, & by the grace of GOD, I was fortunate enough to see Donald as he lay in a hospice in the Bronx. He was granted an early release from prison because he was terminally ill. I was overwhelmed by sadness when I walked into that room. He wasn't able to talk or make loud sounds and I believe he lost his sight. I called out his name & said "it's Tonia". He mouthed my name and held his arms out for a hug, which made me feel good. I was glad he knew I was there. It instantly hit me that the next time he left that room it would be in a body bag.

Donald died in July 2009. The only reason I put this in the book is to remind ya'll how short life is. That's why it's important that if and when you have people in your life that you know love you, you need to stick by them and stay in touch with them. Life is not about using people for your own benefit. It's about being genuine. It's not about the glitter and gold.

How many of ya'll are dealing with someone that you feel truly has your back and cares about your wellbeing? Are they there for the money? My ladies, is he there just to have some where to lay up and get his dick sucked? Some of ya'll already knew the answer before I asked.

Anyway, I can't see myself wasting time on people that don't have my best interest at heart. We all get one life and one chance to make the best of this thing here. Like my ex brother-in -law Billy Sims said "I don't know anybody that died twice." I cracked up when he said it, but it's so true.

We have to take care of ourselves and each other. That's all.

Me and Donald

That Shiny Suit Dude

Okay, remember the dude from Harlem I told ya'll about that had the problem with Maine, right? Well that's Shiny Suit dude. This is the only way I could describe this dude. Well, I could say his name, but nah. LMAO. I already told you that me and him were friends. One day, before all the drama, I bumped into him while I was walking towards Lenox Ave. He had already made it in the rap game and even had his own label. He put together a group from Harlem that included him and four or five other people. I'm sure ya'll saw him in the videos with those shiny suits on. Anyway, we walked and talked and he expressed how mad and torn he was because some of his so called friends thought he owed them something because he was a celebrity.

"Don't worry about that," I told him. "You don't owe anybody anything."

I understood where he was coming from. He wanted Harlem to be proud of him, and we were, but there were some who wanted more. He said that every time he came back to the hood he was greeted by friends who had their hands out. He just wanted to chill with them like old times. He couldn't understand why people changed. He wondered where they were back in the day when he needed something. He told me that the only person who had ever done anything for him was my uncle Stan, who had bought him a pair of sneakers to play basketball in back in the day. He told me he would never forget that. He felt betrayed by his friends. He had a family to support and wanted his friends to understand that.

"You don't owe anyone an explanation. You shouldn't give a fuck about what they think," I advised.

****

Maine was in jail when Lou got arrested and sentenced. I hoped that Maine's seeing Lou on the front pages and learning that Lou got sentenced to 30 years plus the electric chair would change his mind about how he handled business in the street. Unfortunately, it excited Maine even more. I thought the idea of possibly losing his freedom for the next 30 years and being on death row would make Maine see the light. It didn't. Maine had to do him. He got out and it was back to business. My sister had moved on and had a baby and he had a hard time getting over that, but we were still family no matter what.

Maine came home on some Blood shit. I wasn't too happy about that. I always thought that gang shit was for cowards, but Maine was the exception. He was definitely no coward by a long shot. He didn't run with a gang though. He was a one man army. He demanded respect and he got it. It really didn't matter to me what he did. I loved him regardless. He could never do wrong in my eyes. I guess he was going through a phase that started while he was locked up. His presence easily tamed those who thought they were tough.

One day I got a phone call saying that Maine was at a basketball game at Gauchos gym in the Bronx and had snatched a chain off the neck of one of the Shiny Suit dude's rappers. I forgot who called me, but I guess they knew that if anybody could calm Maine down it was me. I always tried my best to keep him out of trouble or calm him down before something bad happened to him. Maine obviously had beef with Shiny Suit dude. I drove over to the gym to see what was going on. I got there and there he stood in the middle of the gym wearing a white t-shirt, red sweat pants and a red bandana. His hair was in cornrows. I'll never forget it. His little skinny ass and big ego never showed any fear.

"What the hell are you doing?" I asked.

"Nah Tee, these niggas gonna respect me. Fuck that. They respected Lou."

I had to remind him where Lou was. Oh and for the record, I was sure it wasn't respect that Lou got in the streets, it always smelled more like fear to me. The gym was packed that day and Maine didn't care that he was standing there alone in a room full of people affiliated with Shiny Suit. A friend of mine, that happened to be a bodyguard for Shiny Suit at the time, was somewhat taken aback by how bold Maine had been. After that day, my sister and I always joked with Maine like, "Yeah MF, you were scared, that day." He would laugh and admit that he was and we'd crack up. That was my nigga though. He was funny as a motherfucker.

The attack against the rapper wasn't personal, but he was on Shiny Suit's team. Shiny Suit's team had gold and diamond dog tags engraved with the label's name and that's what Maine snatched from the kid. Maine wanted Shiny Suit to make an attempt to get the chain back and defend what happened. Just so ya'll know, Shiny Suit wasn't at the gym and I'm sure he wasn't coming after he heard what happened either. I must say, this Shiny Suit shit is hilarious.

I wanted to know why Maine did it. I didn't have the specifics of why he had beef with Shiny Suit.

"I was disrespected," is as much as he would tell me.

I guess he didn't really want me to know what it was. Maybe he thought it would've disappointed me. I found out anyway. Like I mentioned before, there are two things that are not tolerated when dealing with a dude in the streets. Those two things are messing with a man's money or his girl. Apparently, Shiny Suit violated one of those things and Maine wasn't happy about it.

I guess since he had the rap thing going, Maine wanted it to be known that he didn't give a fuck. Maine made it known that if they wanted the chain back, HE had to come get it. Shiny Suit couldn't have imagined what his disrespectful violation would turn into. But Maine wasn't the only one that thought he was tough. Shiny Suit never came out to defend what happened at the gym, but he allegedly sought protection from another tough guy. This guy and Maine already had some tension between them so shit was about to get ugly.

In the meantime, Maine was running around getting the respect he demanded. He was also working his way up to being **That Nigga** in the streets.

Mo Money, Mo Problems

Maine stepped his game up and started selling heroin and it wasn't long before he found himself in beef in the streets. I can't remember the exact date, but I got a call from Maine's cousin, Boogie, in February 1999 saying that there was some drama. Now listen, I'm not getting into everything that happened, which goes for everything I've put in this book. Those who know, know. I don't have time to be called in for any cold cases I know nothing about. I've been under enough investigations and suspicions for bullshit. Ya'll got that? Now follow me. LOL.

Boogie called me and said that some shit went down with some dudes that Maine had a problem with. These dudes ran up on one of Maine's friends and tried to kill him. I'll call that friend Mark. By the way, these dudes were the same dudes that Shiny Suit sought protection from. You see Mark wasn't built like that. Mark was about gettin' money, gettin' bitches and driving fly ass cars. He was a fast talker and funny as hell, but he was not a killer nor a fighter.

So Maine, Boogie, and Mark drove over to the dudes' block to see what was up. I guess the dudes had anticipated the move because they were ready when they got there. Before too many words could be spoken, Boogie and one of the dudes got into a heated argument and shit popped off.

I believe the plan was to get Maine on their block and it worked. By the time I got to 8th Ave, the Wild Wild West had already broken out and ended. Everybody involved was gone. All I saw was a broken storefront glass, Mark's CLK Benz sitting in the middle of the street, police, and people slowly coming out of the wood work wondering what the fuck had just happened. Shit had hit the fan quick.

Somebody ran up to me and told me what went down. "I

think Maine got hit," the person said.

I wondered, "Where the hell could Maine be?" I drove up St. Nicholas Ave because that's where everybody went to elude the police. I figured they ran up that way since it was dark out. When I got up there, police were all over the place searching the area with flash lights. What was about to happen had me buggin' out, but it's true. My cell phone rang and when I answered I heard nothing but moaning on the other end. I saw that it was Maine's number and went crazy. It was Maine's voice.

"Maine?" I kept calling out, but he didn't answer.

All I heard was him groaning in pain. My heart beat sped up and I started to panic. I just prayed that he was okay. The only sense I could make out of this was that I was either the last person he spoke to and he accidentally hit redial or he needed me, but he was too injured to talk. Til this day I don't know what happened, but it was crazy that I got the call. I just listened to him in pain until the phone went dead, clueless of what to do or think.

Boogie called me a while later and told me that Maine was at Harlem Hospital. I rushed over there to find out that Maine had gotten shot 5 times. He was too small to take all that. I just knew it was over. Maybe he would be paralyzed. "Oh God," I thought to myself, "Please let him be alright." The doctor came out and told us that the bullets didn't hit any vital parts. They said that he was going to be okay. GOD was definitely on Maine's side that night.

Apparently when Boogie and one of those guys started arguing, one of the other dudes had gotten really nervous and randomly opened fire, and every shot hit Maine. I heard that the dude that shot him was very remorseful about the situation. He didn't want to kill Maine, but when you're scared you're liable to do anything. He had been scared and just gotten lucky.

I knew that was the beginning of an unnecessary war. For Maine, it solidified his status in the streets. This dude thought he was Tupac for real ya'll. I'm not even gonna lie. I was just like, "Oh Lord!" He already had pictures of Pac on the wall in his room. He started singing that verse from "2 of Amerikas Most wanted" with Pac and Snoop Dog.

"They wonder how I live with 5 shots, Niggaz is hard to kill on my block."

Another verse he liked was from Jay Z's song Streets is watching,

"Look, if I shoot you, I'm brainless. But if you shoot me, you're famous, What's a nigga to do?

LMAO. That was my baby though. Shit was getting real in the streets and Maine had to move. He was starting to make a lot of money and that made him more of a target. He had enough money anyway so moving anywhere wasn't a problem. Boogie told Mark that since all that shit happened over him, he needed to find Maine a safe place to live. Mark had hook ups with a lot of people and places so it wasn't a problem. He found Maine a Condo over in Hackensack, New Jersey. It was nice. He also found an apartment in Yonkers for me and Boogie. Oh yeah, me and Boogie were going together at the time. I forgot to mention that. Yeah yeah. LOL.

We all left Harlem. Well, we didn't really leave Harlem. We just changed our addresses. Yeah, all of that over something so meaningless and there was still no signs of Shiny Suit. It's funny because even if he wanted to squash the beef, he couldn't. It spiraled out of control. I heard that the dudes he wanted to protect him had started pressing his ass too. Maybe they wanted money from him. He created those monsters and now they were on his ass, and yet he was nowhere to be found.

Next thing we heard was that Shiny Suit moved down south. He was retiring from rap and turning his life over to GOD. Ain't that some shit? I guess he needed to repent. Huh? Sometimes we have to be careful what we ask for. He got the hell out of New York on the first thing smoking in fear for his life. But why? Was he running from the same people he enlisted to protect him? Or Maine? Or Both? Why give up your career and leave? Right or wrong? Let's talk about it.

I thought the shooting would slow Maine down a bit, but it just fueled his ego. He got out the hospital and went even harder in the streets. He had to walk around with a sling on his arm for a minute, but that didn't stop anything.

I was hoping things would go back to normal, but what was normal? Maybe that was normal for Maine. It definitely seemed normal for me. Maybe my life was meant to be filled with drama. I just couldn't escape the life of being caught up in crazy situations. I couldn't escape being with and around men who I loved that were caught up in The Life. I had to brace myself because I just didn't know what to expect next.

Those guys that were waiting for Maine that night weren't able to accomplish their goal, but I wondered if and when it was going to happen again. I mean, Maine was hit five times. A lot of dudes got hit once and never made it, but he did. He was very lucky. I was worried that his body wouldn't be able to take it if it happened again. More than that, I knew that if there was another attempt on his life it would be serious. Nobody was really brave enough to approach Maine with beef directly, and whoever did would be as thorough as he was.

Maine

Me, Lil Sis and Maine

NBA Jams

Boogie ended up catching a case over some dope. He was already on parole for life, but they only gave him a year or so to do. I was devastated, but not because he went to jail. He wasn't new to the system, so I knew he would be alright. I was more worried about Maine. Boogie would never let anyone hurt him. You see, Maine was becoming undesirable on the streets to a few people. A handful of people started hating on him because of his rising street status. He was becoming a major street celebrity. All the money he was making didn't help either. But the few that hated on Maine paled in comparison to all those who loved him. A lot of people had lots of love for him. The chicks were going crazy over him. There were dudes that had spent the past ten years hustling on the corner that would never accomplish what he was doing. He was approaching that level in the streets that he had always dreamed of.

That dope game was crazy. Maine was That Nigga in the streets. His name was ringing bells. He and his crew flooded the streets with heroin. The money was coming in by the boat loads. Maine didn't see the big picture of getting out the game at first. He was saving a lot of money, but not to get out.

"Tee when those boys come, I'll be ready," he always told me referring to the FEDS.

He was looking forward to doing FED time. It sounds crazy, but it's true. He actually had money saved up for his next bid. I told him he was crazy and that Lou regretted the situation he was in, but like I said before, Maine had to do him.

That dope was some real serious shit. A kilo of heroin went for over one hundred thousand dollars, and the rewards were even greater when you broke it down and put it on the streets. I'll never forget it. Dope fiends traveled long and far for that "NBA JAMS" and that "TOMMY HILFIGER," which were the names that were on those glassine packages of dope. Maine was supplying just about everybody with that heroin, from East to West, Downtown, Uptown, the Bronx, Queens etc.

One of my exes called me one day and told me he wanted to stop selling crack and fuck with that Boy (heroin).

"You sure you want to fuck with that dope?" I asked.

"Yeah," he confirmed.

I called Maine up, took him to my ex and let them talk like men. My ex called me a few months later and said, "Momi, I ain't never selling crack again." I just laughed.

Now, there were only certain dudes I would've done that for. And it wasn't just because he was my ex. It was because of the way he handled business. I'd known him since the 80's and I knew firsthand that he was game tight when it came to making money. He wasn't on any bullshit. He was very low key and knew how to make money. It's crazy though because as long as dude had been making money in the streets with coke and crack, it was Maine's young ass that put him on in the dope game.

Maine was living the life he'd wanted since he was 15. He wanted to be that dude that people wanted to know. No one would've imagined that that Lil dude was that nigga. He still had that youthful look. I'm not glorifying what he did, but I do admire how he did it. I can't knock anybody's hustle. I feel if you're going to do it, do it big. Do it like Baby Jay did it. Go hard or go home. But of course that was then.

The last king of Harlem was Fritz. He was the richest man in the streets of Harlem before he passed away in 1991. He was responsible for flooding Harlem with cocaine in the eighties. Maine was slowly filling the shoes that Fritz left behind, but there was a difference. Maine loved the spotlight. He loved to be seen.

Maine wanted to get his car game up so he bought a red BMW followed by a S500 Benz, and then a black Cadillac Escalade. His jewelry game was next. He went to Jacob the Jeweler and made a few nice purchases. But with all that flossing came new friends and all sorts of people that just wanted to be around him. Like I said, he loved attention, and especially from the ladies.

No matter who Maine's girl was or what bitches he dealt

with, Lil Sis always had a place in his heart. Some bitches had to find that out the hard way. Like one time we all went on a boat ride and some chick that Maine was dealing with tried to get crazy. I did mention to ya'll before that Lil Sis gets busy, didn't I? Oh yeah, she's the punisher. Long story short, a bitch got punished on the boat, and then Maine punished her too when he found out how shit went down. None of his chicks understood why he still felt the way he did for her after all those years. It's just like me and Lou. True love just never dies. Although they were together when she was twelve the love was still there and we were family. So if you fucked with her, he was getting in your ass no matter what. He loved the shit out of that girl and that's that.

But back to Maine loving the attention. I told him to be careful because all that attention could hurt him in one way or another. In my heart, I knew the worst was yet to come. The more Maine got, the bigger his purchases got. The bigger his purchases got, the more envy I saw in the eyes of those who claimed to be his friends. His next purchase was going to be a Bentley. He was about to kill the streets with that. I remember him telling me he was going to buy it. He told me that he was going to stunt on Dame Dash. For some reason, Maine had a lil problem with that dude, so he was definitely going to show Dame who was really running Harlem. LMAO. That was my baby.

Although he had his lil crew, I worried about him being on the streets without Mike Murder and Boogie to protect him. And when I say I worried, I worried A LOT.

Maine and Boogs

Maine

2000

The year 2000 rolled around and Maine was doing what he did best, making money. The shootouts between Maine and those dudes continued after Boogie went to jail, but no one else had gotten hit until someone close to Maine got hit in the shoulder one night. It was getting dangerous. Maine called me up one day and I met him on the Eastside. We talked and he told me he was getting tired of the streets, the beef and everything that came with it.

"Tee, this shit is getting serious yo," he told me. "I'm not trying to die."

I was so happy to see he realized it wasn't worth it.

"Take your money and just leave the game," I told him.

He had more than enough money to leave the game and be comfortable.

"Why the fuck would you stay around? Just so other motherfuckers can make money? If they can't make it without you then hey," I told him.

My lil man wasn't ready to die ya'll and that's what hurts so much. But sometimes life puts us in situations where we find no other recourse. Shit was getting thick and everybody from the streets knows that murder and drugs don't mix. You have to do one or the other. When you mix the two, things get complicated. It's like mixing bleach and ammonia. There's bound to be an explosion.

I wondered if Shiny Suit realized what was going on in New York or whether he even cared. I'm pretty sure he kept his ear to the streets. I know he was scared and just wanted to forget what he left behind. Maine just wanted to get money, but once somebody on his team got hit, it made things difficult. It got to the point where he felt that he had to handle things in a certain manner. He allegedly put a contract on the head of one of those dudes. I'm sure ya'll have heard the old adage, "There's no honor among thieves." You better believe that shit. You know how they say keep your enemies close, right? Well, those dudes never knew how close their enemy really was. Their own man accepted the contract.

I'm gonna call him Black. Black started hanging on the block with the dudes that Maine had beef with a while before all this began. They knew this motherfucker was no good. He had already robbed and killed a young dude they all grew up with and they did nothing. Now follow me closely here. Allegedly, Black set it up so that those dudes believed he would act as if he would take the bounty. He was supposed to get the money from Maine and then kill Maine after he got the money. That was supposed to be the plan, but it turned out that Black planned on going against his own team all along. Money is definitely the root to all evil.

Black got the money, killed his own man and then joined Maine's team. The streets were buzzing about that shit. Lil Sis and I found out about it just like everybody else in the streets, and we were NOT happy to hear that shit. That was the kind of shit Maine wouldn't share with me until after it was all said and done. It was something I wouldn't have condoned, but being from the streets, I understood that there are times when you feel like your back is up against the wall and there are no other options.

My question was why didn't those dudes go after Black after he killed homie. The MF killed the only thorough nigga from the block after Fifty and they let him walk around like it was okay. I also understand that everybody's not built like that. Everybody's not gangsta, and I understand that too. But those are the kinds of questions that get raised when people associated with The Life don't act or respond to shit accordingly. Meaning, if you really ain't about that life stop frontin'.

Sometimes I wish I could've brought Maine and that dude together. They were two dudes about their business. I could've made them realize that the beef was stupid and all that drama was over that rapper that left them all behind and was nowhere to be found. It was also their egos. No one ever wants to throw in the towel and feel like a loser, but it's not about being a loser. It's about what makes sense.

Just like when Fritz lost those 30 kilos to Alpo, he could've made a decision to start a war, but why when there was so much more to lose. With Maine's business mind and dudes thoroughness, they could've taken over the streets together. But the hate that had grown between the two was just too overwhelming.

If I could rewind time, Shiny Suit could've gone to Maine man to man and explained that he meant no harm in what he did. I often wonder what role Shiny Suit played in all that beef. Did he play a major part in the beef? Was anyone besides Black paid for any services? I'm just asking. I'm sure Harlem wants to know.

On June 23rd, 2000; the boogieman showed up in the darkness on 133rd and 5th Avenue and took the life of my baby, my brother, Jermaine Ragin, aka "Baby Jay." Like I said before, I knew the next time it happened would probably be the last. After Maine's death there were shootouts and all kinds of shit going on. I told ya'll earlier that 6 people died in this beef. I don't know how Shiny Suit feels about that. Maybe he thinks he has nothing to do with it. Who knows? It's fifteen years later and I'm sure he's tried to put it behind him. Did he think it was going to be that easy?

When Maine died, one of the hardest things I had to do was go upstate to see Boogie. We sat and talked about Maine and we cried like babies. I knew if he had been there things may have turned out differently. Maine had people watching his back, but it wasn't the same as having Mike Murder of Boogie around.

If losing Maine wasn't enough, I also found myself under physical surveillance after his death. The police followed me from Harlem to Yonkers for weeks. And then one day, NYPD and Yonkers PD kicked my door in.

Let me tell ya'll how this shit went down. It's actually funny. I lived on the first floor of this apartment building. The entire house was dark except for the TV being on in my bedroom. I saw flashlights moving around outside my window. I peeked through the blinds and saw a bunch of cops walking around in the grass along the side of the building. They had on dark jackets with white letters on the back. I didn't want to turn the TV off because that would've alerted them that I was home. I 2-wayed my ex-boyfriend Donald. Now I don't know why the hell I did that because he would've been just as scared as I was, but he was the only person I could think of because Boogie was locked up.

Anyway, I went into my closet and knocked lightly on the

wall trying to get my neighbor Natalie's attention. Do ya'll know the motherfucking cops were in her apartment listening to my dumb ass? The next thing I knew they were kicking my door in. I flew out the room and ran to the door, yelling, "Wait!" They were like, "Open the door!" I opened it and about ten cops rushed in. There was this one white detective from Yonkers PD that looked like he was about 7 feet tall. They asked for someone from Maine's crew that had never even been to my house. I wondered what the hell made them think he was ever there.

"You got guns in the house?" the detective asked.

"No," I assured.

Get this shit. They told me how long they'd had me under surveillance, described the cars and trucks I drove back and forth to Harlem, and then mentioned some of the places I had been since Maines's murder. It was crazy. I remember thinking, "Maine's gone and I'm still here going through this shit." That's when I knew things had to change, and soon.

It's funny because Maine acted like he was looking forward to a FED bid. It turned out that he was under investigation by the FEDS for about nine months before the boogieman snatched him. DAMN! I wish the FEDS would've come sooner. I could see his little ass locked up, putting a hundred grand in his own commissary, and sending me and Lil Sis money to visit him. SMH! I smile while I write this because I knew him so well.

Me, Lil Sis & Mike Murder

I'm In Pain

Maine's death left me fucked up. I lost weight. I cut all my hair off. I had always sported a short cut, but this was different. I didn't care how I looked. Losing a loved one will always mess you up, but losing that one person that means so much to you can literally make you lose your mind. There is definitely a thin line between having your sanity and losing your mind completely. Remember when Jacob's little brother went on that killing spree after he was killed? That's how it goes when the one that means the most to you is taken away.

It was 2005, five years after Maine died, and I was at the point where New York made me sick to my stomach. I couldn't function and I needed to leave. I had been working as a Property Manager for the past 5 years and had gotten my Real Estate license in August of that year. By the end of the year I realized I needed to get out of New York, but I needed to get my money up before I left.

I called in a favor from one of my dudes that I put on to the dope game. He gave me a few bundles of dope and I set out to do what I had to do. The first thing I had to figure out was where I wanted to sell that shit. I drove around Harlem to places I knew all the fiends hung out and settled on 124th & Lenox Ave. The second thing I did was find a runner. A runner is a fiend that helps you sell your dope, or actually sells it for you. I met this older Spanish dude named Chino. I told him my name was Shay and it was on.

Chino lived in the Bronx, but I had him meet me on Lenox every morning at 6 A.M. I started in the middle of the month of January, 2006. I gave Chino the bundles and then sat in my car, waited and watched his ass work. He worked that block until 9 A.M. That's right, three hours a day. I was in and out. I got out there early enough to make some money and left before it got crazy. Being the first one out got me all that early thirsty money. I sold between 30 and 40 bundles a day. We hit that block until early March. I only needed enough to get out of New York.

My daughter and I had taken a trip to Houston, Texas the previous summer and we loved it. That's where I wanted to move. I didn't have any family there and the only person I knew there was my father's best friend Sonny. Sonny and my father grew up in Jamaica together. My head was so messed up at the time that the fact that I didn't know anybody in Texas didn't matter. Oddly, we found the people in Houston to be very nice and welcoming. I had already arranged for a Realtor to meet with us and take us out house shopping. The homes were nice too and very inexpensive. I was hooked and Texas was going to be my new home. I called Shelli and told her and she was heated. She had already gotten married and moved to Atlanta a few years earlier. She couldn't believe I was even considering living anywhere other than Atlanta. For the past few years, my daughter had spent her summers down there with her anyway.

Once I got the money I needed, I drove to Atlanta that spring and stayed with my cousin Janet for about a month while I searched for an apartment. I found a townhouse apartment with 2 bedrooms, 3 bathrooms, and a back patio. The apartment complex had a gym and a swimming pool too. It was nice. I was in the country and finally had some peace of mind. I was far away from New York, the drama and all the bullshit. I sent for my daughter that August, and we started our lives in ATL. Oh, and let me clear about something. As much as I loved living in ATL, it isn't and has never been a little New York. Never. That comes from people that obviously never been there.

In any event, moving to Atlanta was the best decision I ever made. My daughter got a great education, went to college, graduated, and now has the best career ever. My baby's 23 and holding it down. She pays her own bills, drives a Lexus, and getting involved with The Life is the furthest thing from her mind. I haven't done too bad either. I ended up with two degrees and I'm going on over 15 years in Real Estate.

Yes, I've accomplished a lot despite everything I've been through. So, you see, I am a heroine. I've triumphed by not allowing my circumstances and choices in The Life define and limit my future beyond The Life. I done seen it all in the streets of Harlem. I've been robbed, shot, loss the men that I loved to the grave and the prison system, and I'm still standing, but I'm standing right. I had the strength to overcome my affair with that Harlem Street Life and successfully turned my life around. But like every relationship I've ever had, my relationship with The Life made me stronger. It was a relationship that thickened my skin for whatever else life could throw my way. I'm ready for it all. That's right. I'm not just a heroine, I'm a Harlem Heroine.

Forgiveness

I didn't write this book just to tell stories or call anybody out. This was my life. Shit was real in the streets. I was caught up in the street life and I had to endure the good, the bad and the ugly that came with that life. Like I said before, things weren't always what they seemed. Yeah, I had a lot of good times but I also lost a lot of people that I loved. Sometimes I look back on that life and I'm not sure what to make of it. There are a lot of good memories, but there are a lot of painful memories too. In a lot of ways writing this book has been therapeutic. The truth is that I've been writing it for 10 years. It took that long because I started it and then had a mental block for a few years. I just didn't feel like writing and of course the struggle with the fact that I couldn't put everything in here. At the same time, I wanted to give you enough to get a glimpse of what life in Harlem was for me. Unfortunately, that meant I had to go to some very painful places, the most painful and fresh of which was Maine's death.

But if you never believe anything else, believe this, GOD is the perfect planner in all things and there's no better time to change your life than now. I say that to say that as much as I loved Maine, I eventually acknowledged that the dude that Black killed had people and a family that loved him too. I had been so angry and in so much pain after losing Maine that I overlooked the fact that Maine may have caused those same feelings of pain and despair for someone else. It eventually hit me that I couldn't put my loss above somebody else's loss.

I always understood that The Life brought all kinds of tragedies and setbacks, and Maine's death was a major tragedy and setback for me and his family. I had to charge losing Maine to The Game, to The Life, the life that I loved since I was 15 years old; the life that he loved since he was 15 years old. I know it sounds kind of crazy, but it was that realization that allowed me to move on from all my pain and anger. It took me 8 years to do it, but I did it. And when I say I moved on, I mean I got on my knees one night in my living room while living in Atlanta and forgave the person that killed Maine. I let that hatred go and finally severed my connection to The Life.

If GOD could forgive me for the things that I've done in my life, who am I not to forgive.

I was no longer excited by all the glitz and glamour of the street life. I realized that all the shit that excited me as a young girl was all a façade. I thought that façade was what life was all about, but that wasn't life. At the same time, I'm not mad at the experiences I had in "The Life." They were a major factor in making me into the woman I am today. I'll tell ya'll this too. Façade or no façade, I HAD A MOTHERFUCKING BALL. Yes it gave me a fair share of pain and heartache, but it had its perks too. I'll never forget the parties, yearly trips to Mexico, Puerto Rico, Miami, meeting celebrities, NBA All-Star weekends and flying out to see professional fights. It was a beautiful thing and at the end of the day I'm not complaining. I don't have to call myself the Queen of anything. I've been surrounded by and respected by enough Real Kings and Real OG's in these streets to know where I stood and where I still stand among them. LMAO. No Shade. Unfortunately I couldn't name everybody in here, but they know who they are and what they mean to me.

I would be remiss if I didn't shout out a Real OG. Thanks for your blessing and well wishes with the Book Kenneth "Supreme" McGriff. Stay strong. And yes bending is NEVER an option. Much love.

I just thank GOD I survived all the drama that came with that life and praise Him for keeping me alive to be able to tell about it. I still miss my Lil Man, but I'm good.

One thing I will always do is remain sucker free at all times. Having good character means everything to me. That's what a lot of people lack these days.

I'm good now though. I'm enjoying my life. Oh yeah, I married one of my exes. Ya'll want to know who right? I bet you do. Yep. Life is a funny thing. You never know what can happen, but as I said earlier GOD is the best planner.

Me & Lil Sis

ROYAL-T
PUBLISHING

ORDER FORM

FORMS OF PAYMENT:

Cashier's Checks,
Institutional Checks
& Money Orders

Make Payable To:

ROYAL-T PUBLISHING, LLC
PO Box 600,
NY, NY 10030
royaltypub@gmail.com

Credit Card Payments can be
taken by phone
310-256-3788

$15.00
+ $4.00 S/H

NAME
(Inmate ID# if applicable)

_____

ADDRESS:

_____

CITY/ STATE/ ZIP:

_____

_____

Quantity: _____ Amount Enclosed: $_____

Harlem Heroin(e)

45001638R00117

Made in the USA
Middletown, DE
22 June 2017